Patty Murphy

Piecing

MAKEOVER

Simple Tricks to Fine-Tune Your Patchwork

A Guide to Diagnosing & Solving Common Problems

C&T PUBLISHING

Text copyright © 2016 by Patty Murphy

Photography and artwork copyright © 2016 by C&T Publishing, Inc.

Publisher: Amy Marson

Creative Director: Gailen Runge

Editors: Karla Menaugh and Liz Aneloski

Technical Editors: Sadhana Wray and Debbie Rodgers

Cover/Book Designer: April Mostek

Production Coordinators: Freesia Pearson Blizard and Zinnia Heinzmann

Production Editors: Jennifer Warren and Nicole Rolandelli

Photo Assistant: Carly Jean Marin

Photography by Diane Pedersen, unless otherwise noted

Published by C&T Publishing, Inc., P.O. Box 1456, Lafayette, CA 94549

Library of Congress Cataloging-in-Publication Data

Names: Murphy, Patty (Patricia Priven), 1974-

Title: Piecing makeover : simple tricks to fine-tune your patchwork--a guide

  to diagnosing & solving common problems / Patty Murphy.

Description: Lafayette, CA : C&T Publishing, Inc., [2016]

Identifiers: LCCN 2016000639 | ISBN 9781617452574 (soft cover)

Subjects: LCSH: Quilting. | Patchwork--Patterns. | Patchwork quilts.

Classification: LCC TT835 .M8477 2016 | DDC 746.46--dc23

LC record available at http://lccn.loc.gov/2016000639

Printed in China

10 9 8 7 6 5 4 3 2 1

Dedication

This book is dedicated to my mother, Jennie Priven.
You will always be my greatest teacher.

Acknowledgments

To my friend, Mary Abreu, the Craft Addict. "Thank you" seems inadequate. Your guidance, advice, and friendship have meant more to me than I can ever express. I couldn't have done this without you.

To Roxane Cerda for believing in my idea and helping make this possible.

To Karla Menaugh, Sadhana Wray, and everyone at C&T who helped me create a book I've wanted to write for ten years.

Thank you, Andover Fabrics, Dear Stella Design, Michael Miller Fabrics, and Westminster Fibers, for all the fabric you supplied.

Thank you to Aurifil for sending me your amazing thread.

A big thank-you to Sarah Phillips at Intown Quilters for letting me teach at your shop and for all your support. I'm lucky that you took a chance on me so long ago.

To the cheerleaders, old and new, that I always have surrounding me: Hope Goldberg, Merry Bentley-Barlow, Hannah Burke, Ingie Derouin, Elizabeth Durel, Amy Higgins, Jacqueline Johnson, Callie Kaiser, Marnie Katz, Kendra Sanderson, Lauren Surden, and Ro Lawson. Your words of encouragement never fell on deaf ears. I love each of you dearly.

To Taffy McLaughlin for being such a great mentor over the years.

To my mother-in-law, Claire, for all your support and encouragement.

To my dad, Mike, for always encouraging me to follow my dreams, and to my sister, Laura, for never wanting to learn how to sew.

Most of all, to my husband, Mike, and our boys, Sean and Quinn, for tolerating all the missed meals, dirty laundry, and late nights while I wrote this book. I love you!

Contents

Preface

My mom taught me to sew when I was six years old, and she helped me make my first quilt when I was eighteen. I was immediately hooked and put aside dress patterns to devote my sewing time to making quilts. While my first quilt seemed perfect to me at the time, I now realize it was full of mistakes.

As my confidence and ability progressed, the problems I encountered changed: how to avoid chopped-off points and bulky seams, how to appliqué points and handle curved seams, and so forth. I figured out how to solve the problems I had with my piecing. Often I read a great tip here or there, picked up ideas from other quilters, or just spent time problem solving for myself. My seam ripper and pin catcher became my good friends. They still are.

Thirteen years ago, I stumbled into what was then a new quilt shop just around the corner from me, Intown Quilters. Soon I was fortunate enough to work there and teach classes. I discovered that many new quilters struggled with the same learning curve I faced. I spent countless hours telling students and customers at the shop how to piece better. For them, the results have been amazing, and the experience left me wondering why no one had written a book about how to solve these problems. Knowing these tips can be a huge confidence booster!

This book is the culmination of many years of experience in fixing sewing and quilting mistakes. It's the "Secret Society of Quilters" knowledge—all the little tips that will make your piecing easier. The solutions to piecing problems described in this book are methods that have worked for me. They may or may not work for you. Remember to be creative to find your best solution. Nothing is off-limits.

Happy piecing!

How **to** Use This Book

Determining what makes a great quilt is different for everyone. Most quilters agree that one important element of every beautiful quilt is impeccable piecing—square blocks, perfect points, little or no bulk in the seams. How do you get there? Practice, of course, trial and error, and learning a few tricks along the way.

This book will show you how to use a few basic techniques to solve common problems in construction issues for a wide variety of quilt blocks. It will help you build a foundation of skills that you can apply to many different quiltmaking situations. Some techniques are helpful to know before tackling something new—for example, perfectly pieced strip sets make Four-Patch and Nine-Patch blocks a breeze, and often several techniques can be incorporated into piecing one block.

I hope this book will help you look at blocks differently. Piecing methods are versatile, and there are different ways to construct a block. If a method works for you, then it works. Templates can be substituted for rotary-cut pieces, and half-square triangles and quarter-square triangles can be used in a myriad of ways. Let your creativity flow; experiment or dissect a block to make it easier to piece.

Once you have the basic skills, you can make up some of your own rules. This may inspire you to develop your own technique for piecing a block. The only limit to solving a problem is you. The goal is to reach past your quilting style (for example, it's not about modern or traditional) and focus solely on technique, making your piecing perfect, or at least making you feel less frustrated.

Basic
TOOLS

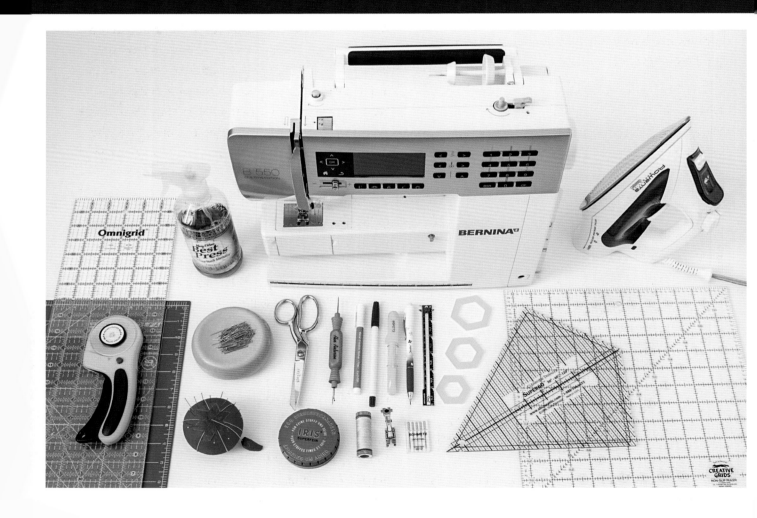

You will need the following tools
to complete the projects in this book.

SEWING MACHINE

You do not need a fancy sewing machine to piece a quilt. The sewing machine only needs to sew a straight line. If you are just starting to make quilts, buy the best machine you can afford. If you find that you like quilting, you can always buy a fancier model later. Many dealers sell refurbished machines that are affordable and work well, but newer, more expensive machines are easier to work with, have a variety of features, and will give you consistent results. Until recently, I'd been sewing on a twenty-year-old BERNINA 1530. I will say, however, that my new machine (read: a newer hand-me-down BERNINA from my mom) is amazing, easy to use, and has features I didn't even know I needed.

Needle down is my absolute favorite feature! It allows you to stop stitching in the middle of a seam with the needle in the down position, going through the fabric and through the throat plate. It holds your work in place, so it's really helpful at corners, for machine quilting, or if, like me, you have small children underfoot. You can stop sewing without losing your place, then continue with a smooth line of stitching.

A complementary feature to needle down is the knee lift, which allows you to raise or lower the presser foot while keeping both hands on your work. The knee lift is a lever that extends from the machine to knee height. Pressing your knee against the lever lifts the presser foot and, if you are using the needle-down feature, keeps the needle down to hold your work in place. I don't always use this feature when I piece, but I couldn't live without it when I machine quilt.

Another of my favorite features is the ability to tap on my foot pedal once to lift the needle from my fabric. I use the foot-pedal feature almost as much as I use the automatic thread cutter and the knee lift. I don't, however, use the automatic thread cutter when I'm quilting. I like to bring the threads to the top so they won't bunch up on the back and I can bury them later.

If your machine has been unused for a while, it's a good idea to take it to a local repair shop to have it serviced. The investment you'll make will be worthwhile because you will encounter fewer problems along the way. Many problems are user error, but not all of them! You will never regret having your machine in tip-top condition when you begin.

¼" PRESSER FOOT

You can follow all the techniques described in this book without a ¼˝ presser foot. I go into detail about how to use that foot, or make adjustments if you don't have one, in The ¼˝ Seam (page 15).

Many newer machines come with a ¼˝ presser foot. If yours doesn't and it's in your budget, I would suggest making the investment. It does make piecing a lot easier.

IRON

An iron is one of the most important tools in your quilting space. There are a lot of different irons on the market. When choosing an iron, you should consider factors that are important to you: its weight and price; how smoothly it glides; and features such as spray, steam control, anti-scaling, and so forth. All steam irons have a water tank and the ability to adjust the temperature for a particular fabric. Read the owner's manual to find out what kind of water you should use in your iron. Some irons can be filled with tap water and others need distilled water. Filling the tank with the wrong water in your iron can ruin it. When you begin a project, make sure that your iron is on the proper fabric setting. If it is too hot, it can scorch the fabric. Scorched fabric smells awful, and you can't always remove the scorch mark.

Tip You can try to remove scorch marks with hydrogen peroxide. Put some hydrogen peroxide on muslin or a spare piece of fabric. Place the fabric over the scorch mark and iron (make sure the iron is not too hot). You may have to repeat the process a few times but it usually gets out the scorch mark.

MARKING TOOLS

Every quilter has a favorite marking tool: chalk, an air-soluble pen, a water-soluble pen, or a pencil. A wide variety of tools are available to mark your blocks and quilts, and some tools work better for a particular project than others. Experiment to find out what you like best. Remember to always test your fabric with a marking tool before you begin. From time to time a marking tool will leave behind the line you drew. A few minutes to test how you are going to mark will save you from agonizing over ruined pieces.

Chalk is great for small projects. The chalk wheel is precise, and you can brush the chalk off quickly. I recommend chalk if you have only a few pieces to sew together because the chalk lines brush off your fabric easily. Most chalk lines are barely there by the time I've sewn on top of them.

Air-soluble markers work well if you need lines marked for a day. The lines will fade, so if you need something marked for a project that you will be working on for several days, a water-soluble marker may be a better choice. Water-soluble pens will leave marks on your pieces for several days or weeks, and will wash off with water. When using air-soluble or water-soluble markers, it is important to remember that even though the lines have faded or been "washed away," the ink is still there. Remove water-soluble marks with cold water, and avoid exposing the markings to heat (iron, radiator, heat vent) because you may set them by mistake.

Water-soluble marking pencils come in several colors, making it easy for you to pick one that will show up on your fabric. I sharpen the pencils to a fine point and then carefully draw the lines to mark the pieces. To avoid damaging the fibers, don't use too much pressure and sharpen your pencils frequently.

Tip My absolute favorite tool for marking lines is bar soap. My mom showed this trick to me years ago. When a bar of soap gets down to a nub, I take it from the shower and put it in my sewing cabinet. The pieces are small and easy to store, and the soap washes out of my quilt pieces!

NEEDLES

Needles are labeled with European and American sizing. The larger number is the European size, and the smaller number is the American size, for example 80/12. The larger the numbers on the package, the bigger the needle. When picking a needle for your project, it's important to consider the fabric you'll be using as well as your thread choice. I do the majority of my piecing with an 80/12, but I paper piece with a 70/10. While needle choice comes down to what you like best (I know many quilters who sew with a 90/14), remember that if you use a needle that is too large for a particular fabric, your fabric may get pushed into your machine. Likewise, if you sew with a needle that is too small, you could break it.

Just as there are many sizes of needles, there are many different types of needles: universal, ballpoint, quilting, double needles, and so on. A universal needle is a good all-purpose needle for piecing quilts, and it will easily go through woven fabrics. A quilting needle is specifically made for piecing and quilting, and will go through multiple layers of fabric. Ask your local dealer or read the user's manual to find the best needle for your machine. Certain brands may be recommended for your machine, and other brands may not work for your machine.

Needles dull faster than you'd think, and a dull needle can rip your fabric, shred your thread, and cause uneven seams. A good rule of thumb is to change your needle after every six hours of sewing and when you begin a new project. I like to dust and oil my machine when I change my needle. It keeps all the parts moving smoothly and keeps my machine relatively lint free. Be sure to check the user's manual or talk to a dealer for information about oiling and dusting your machine properly.

Tip I use a small paintbrush to clean my machine. It gets the dust out and won't cause rust. Buy brushes at a local craft store when they are on sale, and have several different sizes on hand to reach different parts of your machine. I caution against using canned air to clean machines, especially machines with electrical panels. The "air" gets so cold it condenses and can rust your machine, leading to expensive repairs.

PINS

There are a lot of pins on the market—glass-head pins, butterfly pins, silk pins—and they vary in size from extra-fine, fine, silk, and super-fine to relatively thick. Manufacturers label pins differently. Extra-fine for one manufacturer may be super-fine for another. Pin packages should be labeled with the pin size in millimeters, making it easy to pick up another package if you know your favorite size. You can also take pins out of the package and roll one through your fingers to figure out if it's the pin for you. Use whatever you like best, though some pins are better suited for projects than others.

If you aren't sure what you'll like, buy a few different types and experiment. I use silk pins for the majority of my piecing. They are extra-fine, so they don't leave a big hole in my fabric. I buy silk pins without heads so I can iron over them without worrying about melting the pin head. I use longer, slightly thicker glass-head pins if I have to go through something more substantial, and I paper piece with flat-head pins. Whatever pins you use, remember to throw out any that are bent or rusted.

Not all pins rust, but some will. It's a good idea to remove pins from projects promptly to avoid staining your fabric. Rust stains are almost impossible to remove, and rust removal products that are too harsh for fabric can ruin a quilt.

Tip My mother taught me to place pins in fabric so the pin head will be to the right of the needle. If you are left-handed, you may prefer to place pin heads to the left. That way, the pins are hard to miss when you are sewing and easy to remove. Just make sure you keep your pincushion close!

PINCUSHIONS

Whether you use a magnetic pincushion, an emery-filled cushion, or a wool pincushion, you'll need at least one. I have five: two magnetic, one emery-filled, an emery-filled strawberry, and one wool. Magnetic pincushions easily grab pins and are especially useful for picking up spilled pins. Emery-filled pincushions help sharpen and polish pins. And wool pincushions? Well, mine was made by a friend, and I love to look at it. Bonus? The lanolin helps keep needles from rusting.

CUTTING MATS AND ROTARY CUTTERS

You can buy different sizes of cutting mats and rotary cutters. A 24″ × 36″ self-healing mat is my favorite because you can easily cut a full width of fabric that has been folded once. Rotary cutters come in different sizes, too. I have three sizes of rotary cutters for different applications. A 28 mm rotary cutter is great for tight curves. I use a 45 mm rotary cutter for smaller projects and to trim paper piecing. A 60 mm rotary cutter will cut through multiple layers of fabric and is the workhorse for most of my quilting. Be careful when using a rotary cutter. The blades are razor-sharp. You can seriously hurt yourself if you aren't paying attention.

Rotary cutting blades will dull with use. When you notice that your blade isn't cutting through all the layers of fabric, it's time to change it. Dull blades are still sharp, so use caution when changing them. If you want to reuse your old blade instead of buying a new one, you can buy a sharpening tool made especially for rotary blades.

Tip I keep an old, labeled rotary blade case in my sewing cabinet. It's marked USED in large, black letters, and I put my used blades in it. When the case is full I can safely throw it away.

RULERS

I would be lost without my rulers. They come in a wide variety of sizes, from small to large. If you are just beginning to quilt, I recommend buying a 6″ × 24″ ruler first. It will get the job done for most projects. I've had mine for twenty years, and I use it on virtually every project I make.

If you haven't used square rulers, I highly recommend the investment. They come in most standard block sizes and are an invaluable tool for squaring up blocks. Buy your favorite size or two to get started, and add more if you find you need them. Rulers with lines for 30°, 45°, and 60° angles can be used for many different projects.

For your first square ruler, I recommend a 12½″ square. It's a common size and won't be cumbersome when you square up smaller blocks. Remember, it's easy to square up a 6″ block with a 12½″ ruler, but it's impossible to square up a 12″ block with a 6½″ square ruler.

SCISSORS

I keep paper scissors, fabric snips, and a good pair of fabric scissors in my sewing area. Paper scissors are great for cutting paper-piecing patterns and appliqué patterns. Thread snips have smaller blades and are good for detail work or for cutting small pieces of thread as I work. Invest in at least one good pair of fabric scissors. The scissors should be about 7″ long, and they should fit comfortably in your hand. I have two pairs that my kids and husband know not to use, but I keep them hidden

anyhow. Never use your fabric scissors to cut paper! If you plan to cut through multiple layers of fabric with scissors, tailor's scissors with a longer, stronger blade are a good choice.

Did you know you can sharpen scissors? Blades get dull, and many dealers and shops offer scissor-sharpening services for a small fee. I take my scissors to a cooking store to get them sharpened if I can't make it to the quilt shop. You'll be amazed at the difference!

SEAM GAUGE

Mainly considered a dressmaking tool, your seam gauge can help in a variety of ways. If you need to move your needle one way or another, the seam gauge is small and flat enough to get under your presser foot when you need to measure the distance from the needle to the edge of the fabric.

You can use a seam gauge to hold down small pieces of fabric if they start to curl up or move under your presser foot as you sew. You can also use it to measure seam allowances on small bits of fabric. It's easier to measure ¼″ with a seam gauge than with a large ruler or tape measure.

SEAM RIPPER

The tool for unsewing. I use mine all the time. The sharp point will get between stitches and the sharp blade will cut unwanted stitches from seams. As frustrating as it is, don't be afraid to use your seam ripper.

I have three. I keep one next to my machine, one on my cutting table, and one on my ironing board. I am up and down when I sew, and if I have a seam ripper at each stop in my sewing triangle, I save time and aggravation.

When using your seam ripper, remember to keep the ball point down to avoid damaging your project, and take care not to pull the seam apart as you take out stitches. Pulling can distort your pieces, resulting in more aggravation. Ideally, place your project on a flat surface while you take apart the seam.

Tip I have a "third time's the charm" rule when I'm piecing. I'll try to get a seam or point perfect three times. After that, I stop. I feel that gives me ample time to correct the mistake. Chances are, by the third time, it's perfect!

I've always loved my small BERNINA seam ripper. It cuts threads well and fits nicely in my hand. Recently, I started using Alex Anderson's 4-in-1 Essential Sewing Tool (C&T Publishing), which I adore! It has a BERNINA seam ripper, a stiletto, a burnishing end, and a pointed end you can use for turning corners and getting into small places. It's a little larger than some seam rippers, so if small seam rippers cause discomfort for your hand it's a great option!

All fabrics come with a finish that makes them crisp and easier to cut and handle while piecing. If you prewash your fabrics, you will remove the finish applied by the manufacturer. Many quilters prefer not to prewash so the fabric will retain its hand, but what if you do like to prewash *and* you prefer a stiffer fabric? You use starch.

A lot of quilters find that applying starch, or a starch alternative like Best Press, is helpful when cutting and piecing because starch stiffens the fabric so your pieces won't shift as much. Starching fabric can help control bias pieces, and many quilters feel that starch lets them get sharper points and crisper seams. If you decide to use starch, use it on all the fabric in your quilt for consistent results. You can wash the quilt after it is finished to remove the starch.

I prewash all my fabrics and don't use starch unless it's absolutely necessary—for example, if I am working with a loosely woven cotton or lots of bias pieces. After some bad experiences, I have learned how to avoid common problems of working with starch:

- I created flakes because I pressed wet starch; I should have flipped my fabric over to press the back of the starched side, or waited a few seconds until the starch was fully absorbed into the fabric.

- I pressed my fabric incorrectly and distorted a good bit of material. You should try to press along the grain to avoid that problem.

- I starched my prewashed fabric and stored it in a cabinet, attracting silverfish and leaving bad creases in my fabric.

I got so frustrated with starch that I stopped using it. I'm wiser now but still prefer not to use it because I don't care for how it feels.

Using starch is a personal preference and there is no right or wrong answer, just what's right for you. If you aren't sure about using starch, experiment a little. There are some great products on the market and your scraps make perfect test subjects. Make a few blocks to see if you find it helpful.

Tip If you use starch, lower the setting on your iron. It's very easy to scorch starched fabric.

You can't make a quilt without it. Thread comes in a variety of sizes. The lower the number on the thread, the thicker it is. I like to piece with 50-weight 100% cotton Aurifil thread. I like the weight, and seams I sew with it are always flat. I match my thread to my project and use a lighter thread if I can't quite match my fabric. You can also piece quilts with different thread on the spool and in the bobbin. If you are making a quilt with a wide variety of colors, or high contrast, it's a great way to make sure your thread colors blend better and don't peek through the fabric on one side. There are a lot of great threads on the market, so try a few to find what you like best.

Tip The more strands you can fit through the eye of a needle, the finer the thread. Visualize the difference between an 8-weight perle cotton and a 50-weight cotton thread. You'll never forget how thread is sized again!

Use thread that is a shade lighter so you can easily find stitches for "unsewing". An exception would be if you are making an all-white quilt—in that case, go a shade darker and use an off-white or cream-colored thread so you can find the stitches.

NOTE: I used contrasting thread for the samples in this book so you can see my stitches.

Cutting AND Sewing

The ¼˝ Seam

Whether you are new to quilting or have been quilting for a long time, you know that quilters use a scant ¼˝ seam allowance for piecing. The ¼˝ seam allowance has just enough fabric so your blocks don't fall apart, and it is small enough to add minimal bulk to the quilt. But what exactly is a scant seam? Well, it's a seam that is just shy (like a few threads) of being ¼˝. That's important, because once you sew the seam and press it, the piecing thread and the fold from pressing will replace the thickness of those few threads, and the seam will be a perfect ¼˝ in the finished unit.

Consistently and accurately sewing with a scant ¼˝ seam allowance is the best quilting tool you have. There are ways to make sure you always have that perfect seam allowance.

As a general rule, if you are sewing quilting-weight fabric with a thin thread, such as 50-weight Aurifil,

you can rely on your machine's ¼˝ setting to give you the results you want. However, when I work with thicker fabrics or a different thread, I make sure my seam allowance is correct before I begin. The best way to make sure you have an accurate seam allowance is to sew a ¼˝ seam on a scrap of fabric and measure the seam allowance after you press it. You can move your needle to the right or left, or keep it where it is, depending on what you find.

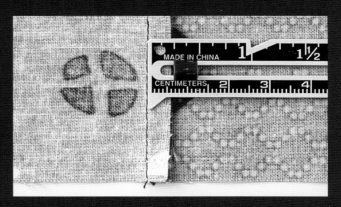

If I adjust my needle for the seam allowance, I usually test with one seam. If you are concerned that one seam won't give you accurate results, sew three strips together so you can really see how accurate your seams are once they are sewn. Your ruler won't lie!

In addition to checking your seam allowance, measure the block itself or the portion you've pieced so far. Measuring at each step of the way will help you get the ¼″ seam you need and improve your overall accuracy.

WHY YOU TEST YOUR SEAM ALLOWANCE

I've had students ask me if testing the seam allowance is really worth the headache. The answer is yes. Being ¹⁄₁₆″ off on one seam is no big deal, right? For one seam it's not, but what if you had eight seams? The ¹⁄₁₆″ error becomes ⅛″ after the seam is pressed open. Multiplying 8 × ⅛″, you'll find you are 1″ off! That's a significant difference, and you may not be able to compensate for a 1″ deficit. Small errors can add up, and using a scant ¼″ seam allowance can help you get the correct size finished block. So always test. You'll thank yourself.

> **Tip** Practice makes perfect. If you are having trouble piecing an accurate ¼″ seam, cut up some old or inexpensive fabric and practice sewing a ¼″ seam. You'll be amazed how a few hours can improve your accuracy and consistency!

Many machines come with a ¼″ presser foot. If yours does not, I recommend that you buy one because it's an invaluable tool for piecing. The edge of the fabric lines up with the edge of the foot, giving you a perfect ¼″ seam allowance from the needle to the edge of your fabric.

If you don't have a ¼″ foot, you can move your sewing machine needle to the right and line up the edge of your fabric with the edge of the presser foot.

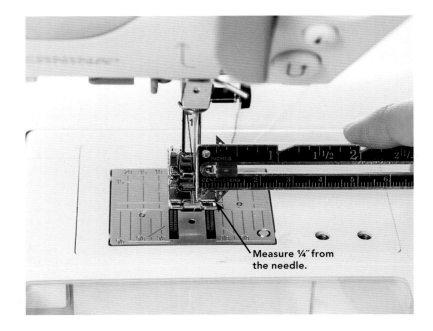

Measure ¼″ from the needle.

If you can't adjust your machine's needle position, you can place a piece of masking tape as a guide on the throat plate. Place the left edge of the tape ¼˝ from the needle. Measure with a seam gauge, which is small, flat, and easy to place under the presser foot. If you can, remove the presser foot and measure from the needle-down position.

If you can't change the needle position and your feed dogs are in the way of a ¼˝ tape guide, place tape on the stitch plate in front and back of the feed dogs.

There are other tools available to help you make a perfect ¼˝ seam. If these solutions don't quite work for you, research and find one that does!

Cutting Perfectly Straight Strips

From time to time, you are happily cutting strips of fabric until you realize that one has a vee in it. That occurs if your fabric isn't on-grain, if the fold of the fabric wasn't aligned with the ruler when you cut the strips, or if the fabric shifted. The good news is that it's easy to avoid and you can occasionally use those strips, too (page 20).

What you don't want:

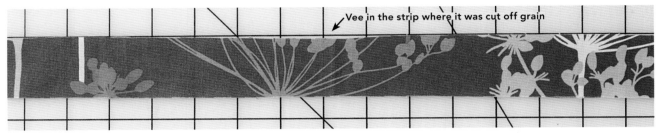

Vee in the strip where it was cut off grain

There is a slight vee at the top of the strip.

Notice that the bottom of the strip is parallel to a line on the cutting mat. At the top of the strip, the vee is gradual but you can see where the strip gets off-grain.

How your strip should look:

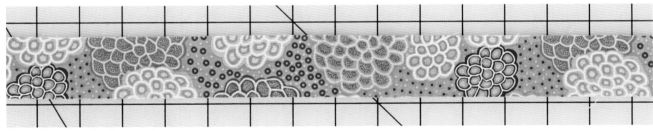

This strip is perfectly straight.

1. To start, fold the fabric with the selvage edges together. If the fabric has a wave in it, then the piece is off-grain.

To get the fabric on grain, I hold the fabric about an arm's distance from me with the selvage edges together. I move the selvage edge that is closest to me to the left and right. When the waviness near the fold disappears, the fold is on-grain, and I can begin to cut the fabric.

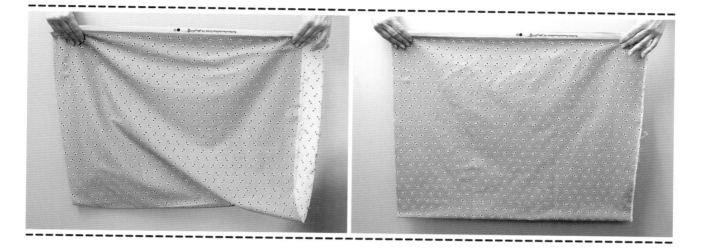

2. Place the folded fabric flat on the cutting mat. I like to place the fabric so the fold is closest to me.

3. Line up one edge of a square ruler with the bottom of the fabric, making sure it's even with the fold of the fabric. Place a 6″ × 24″ ruler along the left side of the square ruler. I try to place the square ruler as close to the left edge as possible; there should be fabric underneath the long ruler, but not enough to be wasteful. I'm right-handed and work from left to right. If you are a lefty, consider working from right to left.

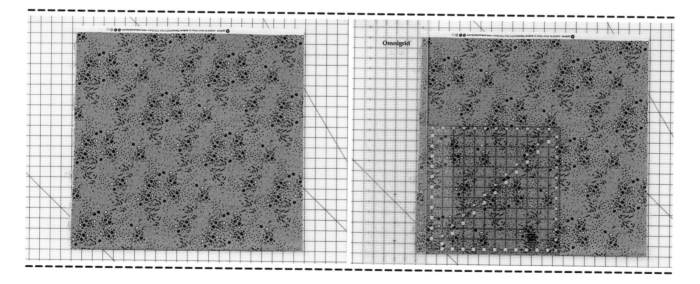

IS MY WONKY STRIP STILL USABLE?

If you plan to subcut squares, rectangles, or other shapes from a single strip, you can usually cut accurate shapes from most of the strip by avoiding the vee at the center.

If I plan to sew a strip into a strip set or use it as a sashing or border, my rule of thumb is that as long as I have an ⅛″ seam allowance at the vee, the strip is usable. Is this ideal? No, but if you have just enough fabric for your project, then this means you won't have to make another trip to your local quilt shop.

1. Place 2 strips together, with the wonky strip on top. Notice the ¼″ line I drew on the strip. Even though the top strip isn't perfectly on-grain, there is just enough fabric for a usable seam allowance.

2. Sew a ¼″ seam.

3. Set and press the seam. Continue to sew more strips, cut these apart, or use them for whatever you have planned for your quilt.

4. Carefully remove the square ruler, and cut along the edge of the long ruler to create a straight cut along the edge of the fabric.

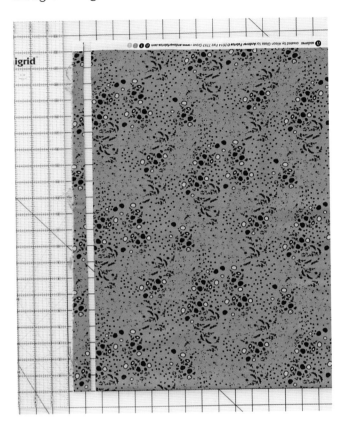

5. Open the strip you just cut. Examine the straight edge. If there is a vee, you need to start over to find the grain. If there is no vee, it is safe to cut strips.

6. Line up the ruler to make a cut at the width you need for your project.

7. Remove the ruler and look at the strip. It should be perfectly straight.

Tip Periodically open strips as you are cutting them to make sure you are still on-grain. If you aren't on-grain, you can refold the fabric to find the grain again, before you end up with a pile of strips with a vee. Remember to cut your strips ½″ wider than the finished size.

Nesting Seams

To nest seams at an intersection, start with two stitched units with seam allowances that fall in opposite directions. For example, to create a Four-Patch block, first sew the pieces together in sets of two, and press the seam allowances toward the darker fabric. When you place the two-patch units right sides together, the seam allowances under the darker fabric will fit together like a puzzle at the nested intersection. Nesting seams at intersections can increase the speed and accuracy of piecing. Some quilters find that they don't even need to use pins if they nest pieces and hold them together as they stitch. I am not one of those people. I pin everything. Nesting at intersections, together with pinning, helps me sew seams that match.

The seam at the top left and the seam at the bottom right fall in opposite directions and nest together at the intersection.

Easing In Seams

In the simplest terms, easing in a seam is making two pieces of fabric that aren't the same size fit together. Easing in seams is common in dressmaking—think sewing a shirt with a set-in sleeve—but the technique easily translates to quiltmaking and is used more often than you'd think. You can ease in seams for blocks, sashings, or borders that are just a little small. You simply pull the shorter piece as you ease in the longer piece so that they fit together. Easing in a seam gives you a little flexibility with your piecing because you don't have to remake or recut pieces that aren't exactly perfect.

To ease a longer piece to a smaller one, put the longer piece on the bottom, next to the feed dogs, when you sew the pieces together on the sewing machine. This step is crucial. When you sew with the larger piece on the bottom, you can pull the top fabric gently as you sew the seam. This process of slightly stretching the fabric is how you ease pieces together.

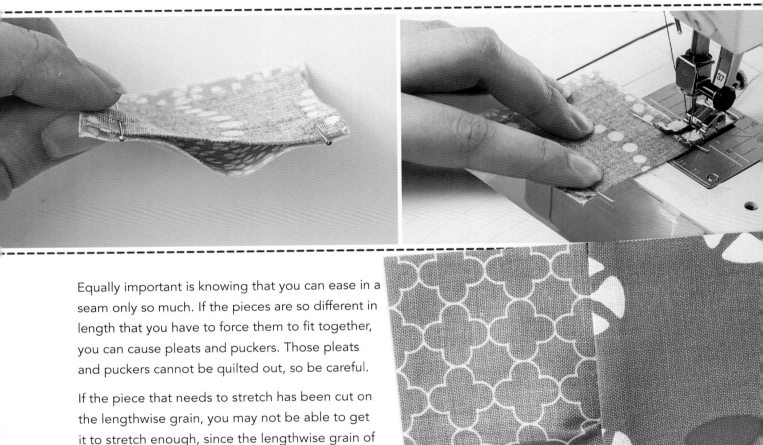

Equally important is knowing that you can ease in a seam only so much. If the pieces are so different in length that you have to force them to fit together, you can cause pleats and puckers. Those pleats and puckers cannot be quilted out, so be careful.

If the piece that needs to stretch has been cut on the lengthwise grain, you may not be able to get it to stretch enough, since the lengthwise grain of fabric does not have much give.

Tip To ease in fabrics, place the longer side, or bubble, on the bottom so the feed dogs will ease in the excess fabric as you sew. A great way to remember how to ease in pieces is with the phrase "keep the bubble on the bottom."

Prewashing Fabric—Yes or No?

Every quilter has an opinion about prewashing fabric. Some prewash, some don't, and fortunately there isn't really a wrong answer.

There are advantages to prewashing fabric. In addition to removing any finishes or sizing that the manufacturer put on the fabric, prewashing shrinks the fabric, usually somewhere between three and five percent. Since different fabrics may shrink at different rates, prewashing ensures that they will not pull your block out of shape by changing after you have pieced them together.

Prewashing also can remove any residual dye from the fabric, helping prevent darker fabrics from bleeding onto lighter colors in your quilt. Don't be fooled, though. Prewashing may not remove all the excess dye in fabric, so take necessary precautions to prevent bleeding. Even though I prewash my fabrics, I put three or four color-catcher sheets in the wash with my quilts just in case. I also stand nervously by the washing machine when the cycle is close to finished so I can put my quilt directly into the dryer and minimize the time that it is folded onto itself in the washing machine.

There are disadvantages to prewashing fabrics. You have to wait to begin your project, and that's a drag when you are eager to start. Once you wash out the sizing, the fabric loses the crisp feel it had when you first felt it on the bolt at the store. For some quilters that's not a problem, but others really like to work with crisp, new fabric. It's easier to cut and maneuver fabric when sizing is still on it. Many quilters compensate for not having any sizing on the fabric by using starch. Another disadvantage of prewashing is that it causes the fabric to ravel, though you can serge the edges or clip the fold like this to minimize the thread madness.

I like to hang my fabric to dry to avoid any tangling from tumbling around in the dryer, but that takes longer. If you put the fabric into the dryer, cut off any badly frayed threads and separate all the pieces before putting them in to minimize tangling.

If you don't want to prewash your fabric, you can feel encouraged by the fact that most manufacturers use dyes that are far superior to what they once were, so any bleeding is minimal. And if you don't prewash your fabrics but wash your quilt when it's complete, you create a cozy, loved look to your quilt.

The only time I don't prewash fabrics is when I am making a wallhanging. The finish on the fabrics protects it from light and keeps it crisp and smooth.

Clip. ➔

Fold the fabric with the selvages together. At both cut ends of the fabric, clip a small 45° vee at the fold to prevent excessive fraying.

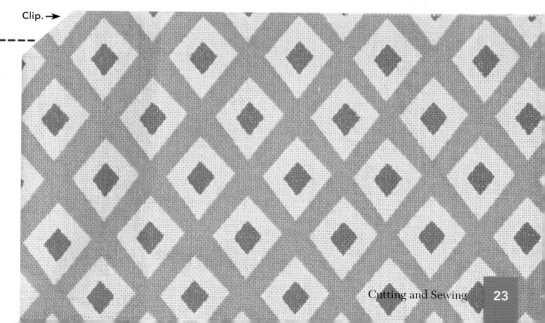

Pressing

Standing at the ironing board pressing piece after piece is dull, but properly pressing your blocks and finished quilts is one of the most important tasks in making a well-pieced quilt. I tell students that it's the difference between handmade and homemade. That always leads to two questions: What is the difference between pressing and ironing, and do I need to set seams?

Pressing versus Ironing

Well, pressing is just that, using the weight and heat of the iron to flatten a seam. You place your iron on a seam; once the seam is flat, you lift and repeat in another spot. When you iron, you move the iron back and forth across the fabric, which causes friction. The side-to-side and back-and-forth motion of ironing (imagine ironing a shirt) can distort quilt pieces or fabric. If you press by lifting the iron and placing it down on a seam, you won't cause distortion in your blocks. If you catch yourself ironing instead of pressing, just stop what you are doing and start again. Chances are you haven't distorted the block that badly, and you may be able, to carefully reverse any damage.

Ironing does have its place in quilting. If a quilt has been folded up for a while, ironing without steam is a great way to smooth it out. I recommend using a pressing cloth when you iron a quilt to keep it safe from accidental scorches. A lightweight, white cotton barkeeper's towel is a great tool to keep in your sewing room. It's light enough for the heat of the iron to penetrate and heavy enough to help avoid any damage to your quilts. Additionally, because the cloth is white, you don't have to worry that it will accidentally bleed onto your quilt. Always be careful when you iron a quilt, but use extra caution when ironing a quilt if you aren't sure of the fabric, thread, or batting content, especially with old or antique quilts.

Setting the Seam

Before you press a seam open or to one side, you need to set the seam. Before you open the fabric, place the iron over the seam and press. Setting your seams will help the thread nestle into the fabric and help with any uneven stitches, giving you a crisper, flatter seam, and thus more precise piecing. It will remove any light puckering in the fabric from when it went through your machine, too. Remember to remove any pins before setting a seam so you don't melt any plastic pin heads.

Notice the difference between seams that are set and seams that are not set.

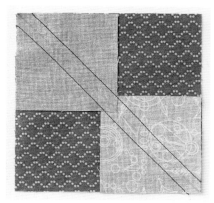

Set seams are crisp and flat.

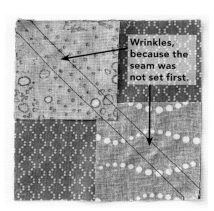

Wrinkles, because the seam was not set first.

Seams that have not been set often have wrinkles.

Tip Make two identical blocks. Set the seam on one block, and then press. Don't set the seam on the other block, and press. Do you see or feel a difference?

Whether to Use Steam

Whether or not you should use steam to press fabric has been greatly debated among quilters. Everyone has an opinion.

I press everything with steam. I like the results better. I get a very flat, crisp seam when I use steam. If you use steam, be sure to leave whatever you pressed on the ironing board to cool so you don't pick up damp pieces and distort them. Believe me, it does happen. Be careful not to burn yourself with the steam, either. That happens, too. Using a stiletto to help hold pieces down can help prevent burns.

A dry iron definitely has its place in quilting, and you can get great results using one. A dry iron is my go-to setting when I use fusible web products or press on appliqué. I'm less likely to make a mess on the bottom of my iron and I won't distort appliqué pieces if I use a dry iron. I know many quilters who use only a dry iron. That's okay. Figure out what you like best and use it.

Tip I keep a spray bottle on my ironing board with a 50/50 mix of water and vinegar. The vinegar helps release stubborn wrinkles in yardage, blocks, and scraps.

Open or Closed? Which Way Do I Press My Seam?

You can do both. It depends on the quilt and the block.

When I started quilting, I pressed everything to one side, always toward the darker fabric. I was making relatively easy quilts, so most of my intersections nested together nicely (page 21) and I didn't have any problems. As I became a better quilter and started making quilts with more complex blocks and patterns, pressing to one side all the time became a problem. I had quilts with a lot of bulk in some spots and intersections that didn't nest together well. I learned that pressing some seams open would improve the quality of my work and the overall appearance of my quilts.

So why should you press seams open versus to the side? A seam from your sewing machine is far stronger than a hand-sewn running stitch, so why not press all seams open? Each method has its advantages, and generally speaking, neither method is wrong. Many quilters have strong opinions about using one method or another, and in most cases that's fine. There are times when pressing a seam open is necessary to maintain the integrity and accuracy of a block, usually when piecing complicated blocks or blocks with a lot of points.

Advantages of pressing seams to one side:

- It helps strengthen the seam because the stitches are covered with extra layers of fabric. If the seam does pop open, the seam allowance is under the seam opening, making it easy to repair.

- Pressing seams to one side makes it easy to nest, or lock together, pieces of your quilt.

- All the fabric falls to one side of the seam, creating a "ditch" on the opposite side. Some quilt-makers choose to quilt in-the-ditch around some or all of their blocks, which gives them a nice

outline. This isn't a compelling argument, since not every quilt needs to be stitched-in-the-ditch, but when seams are pressed open, stitching-in-the-ditch is not an option.

- It's faster and easier to press a seam to one side.

Disadvantages of pressing seams to one side:

- If you don't press toward the darker fabric, you can create a shadow through the lighter fabric.

- Pressing seams to one side can increase bulk in complicated intersections.

Advantages of pressing seams open:

- It reduces bulk, and that can help you sew blocks together. For complicated blocks with lots of points, reducing bulk makes it easier to feed pieces through your machine.

- The overall appearance of your quilt top will be flatter.

- You can see the exact position of every point. This gives you the opportunity to position the pieces properly, making you less likely to cut off a point in the seam allowance. This is a big advantage in blocks like Ocean Waves (page 74) or Equilateral Triangles (page 98), which have a lot of points. This is especially important if you are working with bias pieces.

The more you repeatedly rip out a bias seam, the more likely you are to stretch the piece and get frustrated.

With an open seam, you can line up points exactly.

Disadvantages of pressing seams open:

- You have to take more care to ensure that intersections meet, because you lose the nesting advantage. Make sure you pin carefully before sewing pieces together.

- Open seams are harder to press. I recommend using a stiletto, dowel, old chopstick, or other tool to help hold open the seam as you press so you don't burn yourself.

The best solution is to marry the two methods. Some blocks or quilts need a little of both. As a general rule, if I am matching a lot of points I press seams open, as in Ocean Waves (page 74). But not always, as in LeMoyne Star (page 78).

As you become a better quilter you will learn what works well for you. I encourage you to think about the best way to press blocks before you begin. You might choose the wrong method and have to rip apart a block or two, and as frustrating as that is, it's the best way to learn. Over time you will learn to anticipate the best way to press a block and think it through before you start.

Keeping Your Iron Clean

Whether you are pressing, ironing, using steam or not, one way to ruin quilts or blocks is with a dirty iron. You'll know when your iron is dirty either by looking at the sole plate or by feeling some drag across the fabric as you press. You may even notice dirty water dripping from the bottom of your iron or see it on your ironing board cover.

There are different ways to clean an iron. I buy iron cleaner in a tube from my local craft or fabric store. It smells bad, but it works. I keep inexpensive muslin on hand to help with the job so I don't have to ruin a towel or nice fabric. Just recently I bought a new iron, and it has a self-cleaning function to help descale the inside. Every iron is different, so be sure to follow the manufacturer's directions for cleaning your iron.

Furling Busy Intersections

Furling refers to rolling an item around a center staff, such as a flag around a pole or an umbrella around a handle. To me, it's the perfect word for this pressing technique, in which you rotate the seams around an intersection.

To furl the seams, take out a few stitches in the seam allowance so you can rotate the pressing direction and get less bulk with a flattened seam.

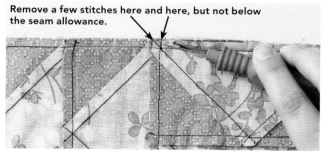

Remove a few stitches here and here, but not below the seam allowance.

Take out a few stitches in the seam allowance.

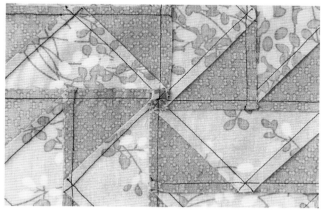

Press open the seam allowances at the intersection.

Furling is a great technique to use when you make blocks with a lot of points, because those intersections include the bulk of the intersection as well as the accumulated bulk from previous seams. Furling a seam promotes a flatter intersection and less bulk. It also means that you pick out a few stitches very close to that intersection, which may compromise the integrity by weakening the seam.

So you have to make a decision: Is a slightly compromised intersection worth the advantages of furling? If I know that furling will make a difference in the appearance and feel of blocks, I will do it. Complicated blocks with a lot of seams at intersections, like a LeMoyne Star (page 78) or a Pinwheel (page 66), benefit greatly from furling. If the block is simple, like a Four-Patch, the tradeoff is not worth it. Sometimes pressing a seam open will give you the same results as furling a seam. In the end, whatever you like best is what you should do.

BUILDING BLOCKS

I've divided this book into several sections, with each section building on the previous one. This section contains classic blocks. They are, in every sense, the building blocks and basic foundation for many quilt blocks and designs you see today, as well as those from the past.

Many of the elements in this section are incorporated into other complicated blocks. Or they can stand alone to add character to quilts, like a checkerboard border. Mastering these basic skills will help you gain confidence when you piece more complicated blocks.

30 Strip Piecing

34 Four-Patch

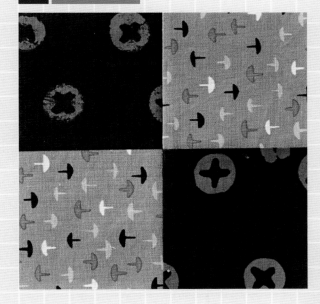

36 Nine-Patch

38 Half-Square Triangle

40 Quarter-Square Triangle

46 Flying Geese

Strip
PIECING

Problem ➤ There is a curve in my strip-pieced set.

What you don't want:

A curve in the strip set

How your block should look:

DIAGNOSIS

Sewing multiple strips together in the same direction creates a curve.

As simple as it seems to sew strips together, there are a few things you can do to make better strip sets. This is important if you make strip sets to subcut for Four-Patch, Nine-Patch, or other blocks. Any curve in the strip set will make nesting seams difficult. If you are using a strip as a filler or coping strip, it will be hard to straighten the curve and you will create a wave in your quilt.

Cut each strip ½˝ wider than the finished size and be sure to sew with an accurate ¼˝ seam allowance (page 15). Alternate the direction you sew the strips to avoid creating a curve in the middle of the strip set. I like to mark one side of the selvage with a *T* for *top* so I don't forget the direction I need to sew strips together.

1. Arrange strips with one end of the selvage edges together. Mark one end of each with a *T*. I mark the selvage edge with the manufacturer information.

2. Sew 2 strips together, starting at the *T* and sewing to the opposite end of the strips. Press the seam. I like to press seams for strip sets to the side, but you can press them open, if you prefer.

3. Sew the next strip from the bottom to the *T*. Press the seam.

4. To sew the remaining strip, start at the top (*T*) and sew to the bottom of the strips. If you have more strips, continue to alternate sewing directions.

5. Press all the seams in the same direction, or open if you prefer.

SUBCUTTING STRIP SETS

1. To subcut units from a strip set, lay the strip set flat on the rotary mat. Line up a square ruler with the seams. Align a long ruler with the left edge of the square ruler.

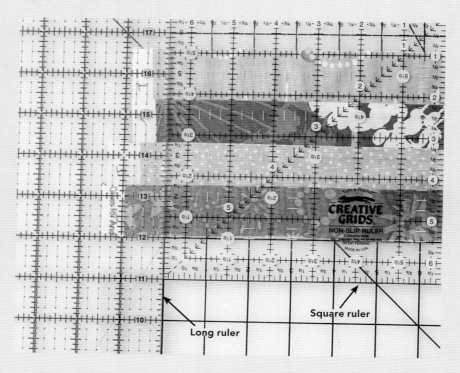

Long ruler

Square ruler

2. Remove the square ruler and cut along the right-hand edge of the long ruler to cut off the excess selvages and uneven strips on the left.

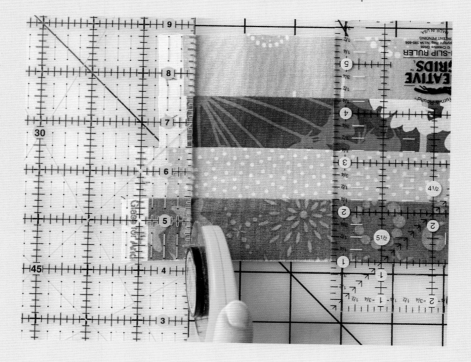

3. Cut the units to the width you need for your project. With each cut, line up the horizontal lines of the ruler with the seams and the top and bottom edges of the strip set.

Tip I'm right-handed. Reverse the strip and rulers if you are a lefty!

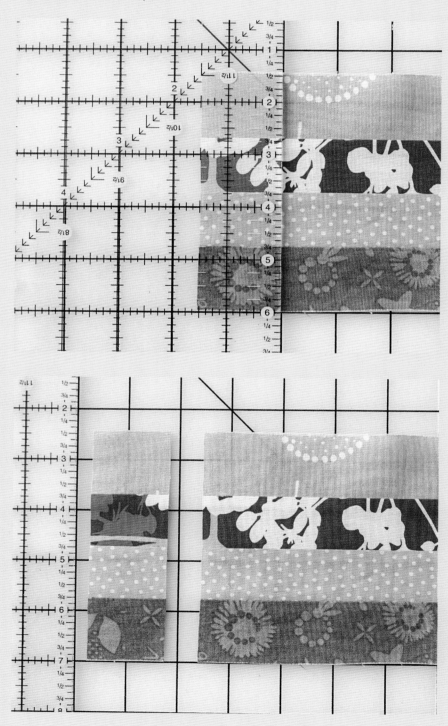

Four-Patch

Problem ➤ My seams don't meet perfectly.

What you don't want:

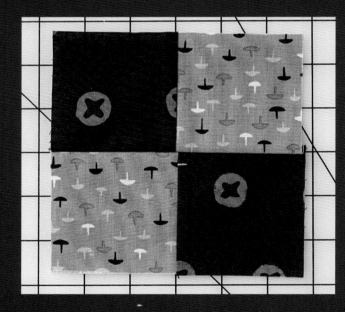

How your block should look:

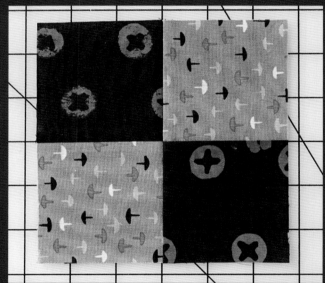

DIAGNOSIS

Sewing an inaccurate ¼″ seam allowance or pressing all seams
to one side can create bulk and seams that don't meet.

I love the ease of putting Four-Patch blocks together when I strip piece (page 30). Usually when you press the seams to one side, they nest together (page 21) as you piece the units, and the blocks turn out nicely. The same is true for Four-Patch blocks that are made without strip piecing from four separate squares of fabric.

However, even with a perfect ¼″ seam allowance and proper pressing, seams don't always meet perfectly. Make sure that you press the seam allowance toward the darker fabric if you can, so your pieces can nest together. I like to use a pin to mark my ¼″ seam allowance before sewing.

Cut the strips and squares ½″ wider than the finished size. For a Four-Patch block that will finish at 4″, you will need four squares 2½″ or strips 2½″ × width of fabric that will be sewn into strip sets and subcut into 2½″ × 4½″ units.

Start with two sets of two-patch units, with seams pressed to one side.

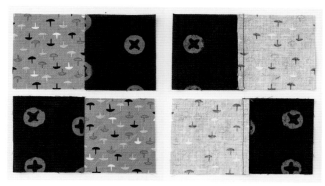

The front and back of a pair of two-patch units

1. Nest the pieces right sides together. Insert a pin through both seams, ¼″ from the top edge. The pin will hold the pieces together as well as indicate the exact position of the ¼″ seam allowance as you sew.

Before sewing, feel the seam to be sure the 2 sides nest together well.

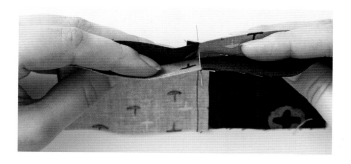

2. As you stitch, make sure your stitching line crosses just a thread or 2 above the ¼″ position marked by the straight pin.

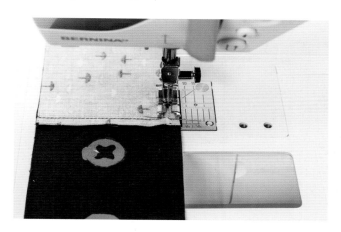

3. Press the seam.

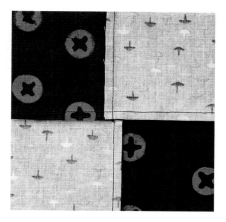

Tip If you struggle with Four-Patch blocks that are too small, your seam allowance is probably a bit too large. One easy way to get accurate blocks is to start with larger strips and cut the block to the proper size after you have finished piecing it.

Nine-Patch

Problem ▶ My seams don't meet perfectly.

What you don't want:

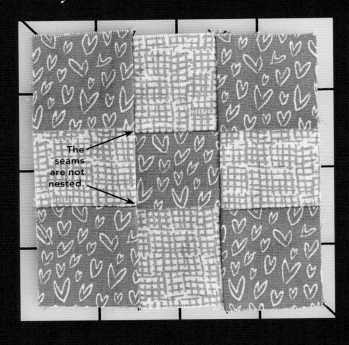

The seams are not nested.

How your block should look:

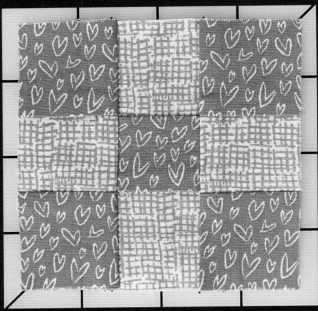

DIAGNOSIS

If you didn't sew an accurate ¼˝ seam allowance on your strip sets or didn't press seams correctly, you could have created bulk and seams that don't match well.

SOLUTION

Sewing accurate and consistent ¼˝ seams and pressing the seam allowance toward the darker fabric will allow you to make perfect Nine-Patch blocks. Make sure you cut strips ½˝ wider than the finished size square.

If you want a 3″ finished Nine-Patch block with 1″ finished squares, you will need to cut three strips 1½″ × width of fabric.

Occasionally, matching all or some of the four points in the center of a Nine-Patch block can be tricky. If you are a little bit off with your seam allowance, you can ease in the seams (page 22) of the block. You also can use a pin to mark the ¼″ point on the seam, just as shown with the Four-Patch blocks (page 34).

For this example I am making Nine-Patch blocks from strip-pieced sets, but you can also make Nine-Patch blocks from nine separate squares of fabric. If you make your blocks in strips, sew three strips of three squares each, making sure to press the seams in alternate directions so they will meet at the intersections.

Often you can feel that your Nine-Patch blocks won't nest perfectly as you pin them together, or you may notice after you have already stitched the seam that they didn't nest. If you have already sewn the seam, carefully remove the stitches, press the parts, and resume making the block.

> **Tip** Press seams toward the darker fabrics to avoid any shadowing through lighter fabrics.

1. Start with 3 rows, each with 3 squares. The finished size of each square should be ⅓ of the finished size of the Nine-Patch block. Press the seams toward the darker fabrics.

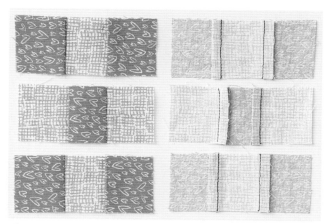

The pressing direction allows the seams to nest.

2. Place 2 rows of the Nine-Patch block right sides together. Shift the bottom of one intersection until the seams nest (you can feel it with your fingers). Place a pin through the seams and repeat on the other intersection. You will have something that looks like this. It may fit perfectly, or it may have a bubble on one side of your block.

Bubble on the bottom

If your squares are far from matching, your sewing may have been a little off. That's okay. It happens. Carefully remove your stitches and resew the units before you stitch the block together.

3. Sew the 2 rows together, making sure you have the bubble on the bottom. When you get to the sections that are mismatched, gently pull the pieces while you sew. This will ease in the bottom piece so it fits with the top piece. Press the seam.

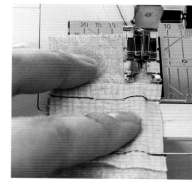

4. Sew the remaining side of the Nine-Patch block, easing in seams if necessary.

5. Press the seam.

Half-Square TRIANGLE

Problem ➤ My block is the wrong size and the seam is wavy.

What you don't want:

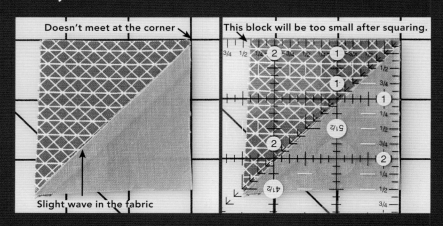

Doesn't meet at the corner

This block will be too small after squaring.

Slight wave in the fabric

How your block should look:

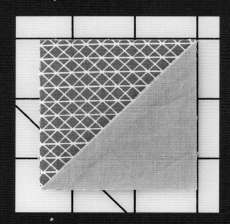

DIAGNOSIS

Sewing on the bias can be challenging. Bias edges stretch and wiggle around while you are sewing, so you can be left with a wave in the seam or a square that isn't quite the right size. Your block can finish at the wrong size if you don't sew an accurate ¼″ seam, and adding fabric to a finished Half-Square Triangle isn't possible.

To avoid those problems altogether, make Half-Square Triangles using larger squares of fabric. Don't cut triangles first. Save that step for last.

Traditionally, Half-Square Triangles are made by cutting squares ⅞″ larger than the finished size of the Half-Square Triangle. For example, 2″ finished Half-Square Triangles start as 2⅞″ squares.

An easier approach is to add 1″ to the finished block size for the squares, and then cut down the block and square it up after you have sewn it. For example, cut 3″ squares to make 2″ finished blocks. Making Half-Square Triangles this way isn't much more work, but it will save you a lot of frustration and improve your speed and accuracy.

1. Cut 2 squares 1″ larger than your finished block size. For this example, I am making a 2″ finished Half-Square Triangle, so I cut my squares 3″.

2. Place the squares right sides together, making sure you match corners. Draw a diagonal line from corner to corner on the top square. Secure the squares with a pin.

3. Sew ¼″ from each side of the diagonal line, making sure you don't sew over the pin.

NOTE: Sewing on a square of fabric provides more stability. You will sew on the bias, but you won't stretch the pieces as much as you would if you were sewing along the cut bias edges of triangles.

4. Set the seam, and then cut the squares in half along the diagonal line.

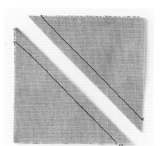

5. Press the half-square triangles open or to one side.

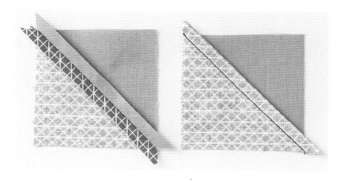

NOTE: Most of the time I press the seam allowance on Half-Square Triangles open. It causes less distortion to the block. For some blocks, like Pinwheels, it is better to press the seams to one side so you can nest (page 21) them together for perfect points. Consider where you will be using the Half-Square Triangle before piecing. One method may work better than the other for your finished quilt.

6. Square up your block. Align the 45° line of your ruler with the diagonal seam for easy squaring. Notice the diagonal seam is perfectly straight, and there's not much to trim to make the block the correct size, 2½″ in this case.

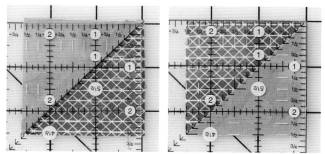

Square up the first 2 sides, and then turn the block around and square up the remaining sides.

Quarter-Square TRIANGLE

Problem → My block is the wrong size, the center seam doesn't match, and the outside edge is wavy.

What you don't want:

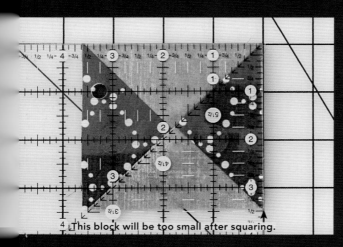

4 This block will be too small after squaring.

How your block should look:

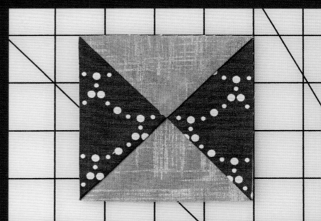

DIAGNOSIS

Just as with Half-Square Triangles, Quarter-Square Triangles are traditionally sewn with the triangles already cut, so you end up sewing bias edges together. Sewing on the bias can cause distortion, and your blocks

Make Quarter-Square Triangles using squares. Sewing diagonally across a square of fabric provides more stability. You will sew on the bias, but you won't stretch the fabric as much as you would if you were sewing along the cut bias edges of triangles.

Cut the pieces for your Quarter-Square Triangles larger and then trim the block to the correct size. Make sure you sew with an accurate ¼˝ seam, and don't cut your fabric into triangles before piecing.

The traditional method to piece Quarter-Square Triangles is to cut squares 1¼˝ larger than the finished size and then cut them in quarters diagonally to make four triangles. If you want a 3˝ finished Quarter-Square Triangle block, then you start with 4¼˝ squares.

I like to cut my fabric slightly larger and trim the block after it's made. Just as with Half-Square Triangles, there is minimal waste and significantly less frustration. I cut my fabric 1½˝ larger than the finished block size.

SOLUTION

1. First, follow Steps 2–4 of Half-Square Triangle (page 38) to make 2 units, using 2 squares that are cut 1½˝ larger than the finished Quarter-Square Triangle block. For this example I cut 4½˝ squares to make 3˝ finished blocks.

2. Press the seams toward the darker fabric.

3. Place the half-square triangles right sides together, making sure the seams nest (page 21).

4. On the top half-square triangle, draw a diagonal line from corner to corner, perpendicular to the seam. Secure the half-square triangles with a pin.

5. Sew ¼˝ from each side of the diagonal line, making sure you don't sew over the pin.

6. Set the seam, and then cut the squares in half along the diagonal line.

7. Press the Quarter-Square Triangles open with the seam to one side.

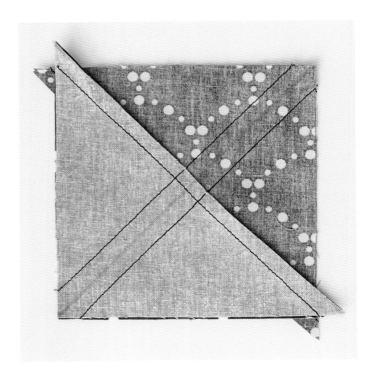

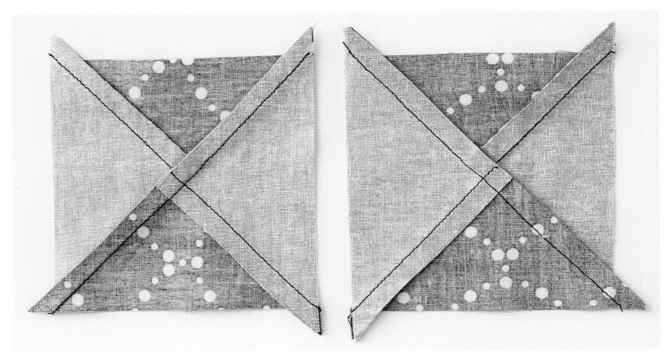

You also can furl the seams (page 27). Gently pick a few stitches from the center seam allowance, rotate the seam allowance around the center intersection, and press.

8. Square up your block. Align the 45° line of your ruler with the diagonal seam for accurate squaring.

To trim the block, use the ruler to line up the center of the block with the halfway point of the unfinished block size. For a 3″ block, the 1¾″ mark is the center (remember, it's 3½″ unfinished).

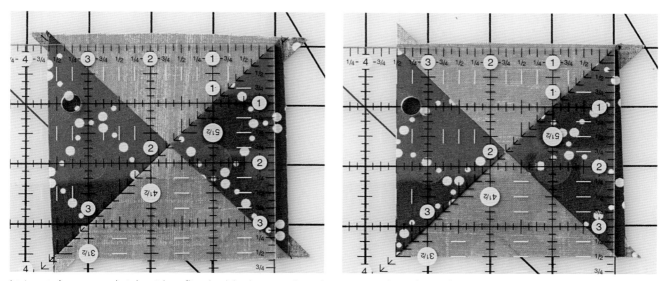

I trim at the top and right sides, flip the block around, and repeat on the other sides to get perfect blocks.

Blocks with Four Fabrics

This method will make four Quarter-Square Triangles, two at a time. To make only two Quarter-Square Triangles, reserve the extra half-square triangles for a different project.

1. Start with 4 squares, 1½˝ larger than the finished size of your Quarter-Square Triangle block. Each square should be a different fabric. Pair the squares together to make 2 sets of Half-Square Triangles (page 38). Press the seams toward the darker fabric.

2. Using a half-square triangle from each set, follow Steps 3–8 of Quarter-Square Triangle (page 41) to complete 2 Quarter-Square Triangle blocks made from 4 different fabrics.

Blocks with Three Fabrics

This method will make two quarter-square triangles at a time.

1. Start with a Half-Square Triangle and a square of fabric the same size; both should be 1˝ bigger than the finished size of your Quarter-Square Triangle block.

2. Place the Half-Square Triangle and the fabric square right sides together, with the Half-Square Triangle on top. On the back of the Half-Square Triangle, draw a diagonal line from corner to corner, perpendicular to the seam. Secure the pieces with a pin.

3. Follow Steps 5–8 of Quarter-Square Triangle (page 42) to complete 2 Quarter-Square Triangle blocks made from 3 different fabrics.

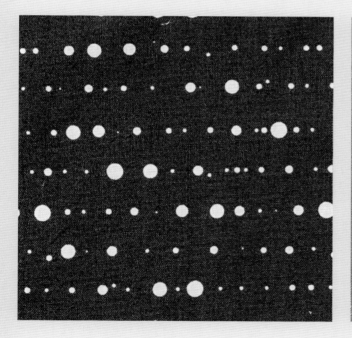

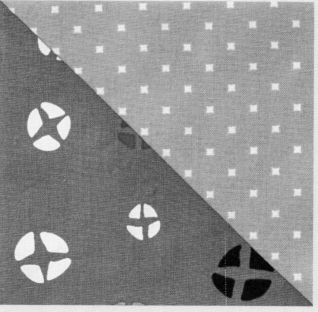

Tip I like to square up the side with two triangles first. It's more forgiving to square up your block on a solid piece of fabric last.

Flying GEESE

Problem ➤
My Flying Geese blocks are distorted and will be too small when I trim them.

What you don't want:

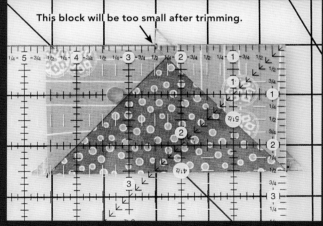

This block will be too small after trimming.

This block is too small, and the edges are wavy.

How your block should look:

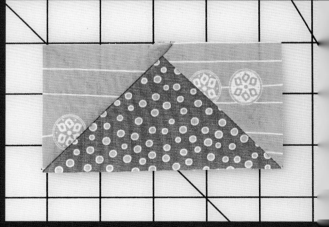

Front of a perfectly sewn block.

DIAGNOSIS

Bias is the likely culprit of wonky Flying Geese, since they involve multiple bias seams. The slightest amount of stretch while sewing can cause distorted blocks.

When Flying Geese are sewn together as three separate triangles, both inside seams are sewn along the bias, which can stretch easily during sewing. I like to create my Flying Geese from squares. I make them oversized and then trim them down to produce perfect Flying Geese.

Flying Geese are made of a large center triangle with two smaller outer triangles. The triangle in the center is one-quarter of a larger square, and the smaller triangles on the outside are each one-half of a square. If you recall the math from the Half-Square Triangles (page 38) and Quarter-Square Triangles (page 40), you'll remember that I add 1″ to the finished size of a half-square triangle and 1½″ to the finished size of a quarter-square triangle. With Flying Geese, you are making half- and quarter-square triangle units, essentially—they are just modified so smaller half-square triangles are sewn onto larger quarter-square pieces.

For this example, I am making 2″ × 4″ finished Flying Geese. Using the quarter-square triangle math for the larger triangle, you add 1½″ to the 4″ finished size to start with a 5½″ square. Using the half-square triangle math for the two smaller squares, you add 1″ to the 2″ finished size to start with 3″ small squares.

This method makes four Flying Geese, two at a time.

1. Cut 1 square 5½″ (this is the "goose") and 4 squares 3″ for the smaller triangles (the "sky") on the sides.

2. Place 2 small squares, right sides together, on opposite corners of the larger square. The squares will overlap a bit in the center. Draw a diagonal line from corner to corner through the small squares. Secure the squares with pins.

3. Sew ¼″ from each side of the diagonal line, making sure you don't sew over the pins.

4. Set the seam, and then cut the pieces apart. Press the smaller triangles away from the larger triangle, forming 2 heart-shaped pieces.

5. Place a small square on the corner of each larger triangle, right sides together. Draw a diagonal line across the square. Secure each square with a pin.

6. Sew ¼″ from each side of the diagonal line.

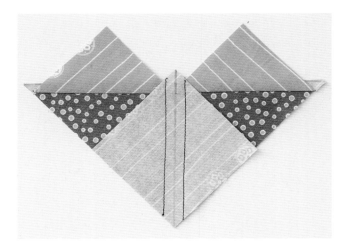

7. Set the seam, and then cut the pieces apart along the diagonal line. Press toward the small triangles.

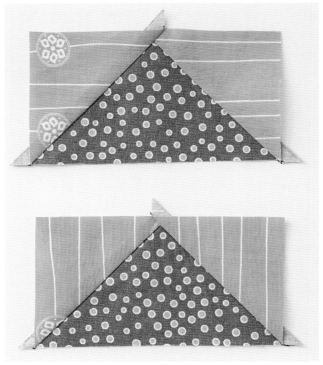

8. To trim the block, find the center point of the height of the unfinished block and line up that measurement with the 45° angle on the ruler. This particular block is 2½″ × 4½″ unfinished, so the center point is 2¼″. Trim across the top and right-hand sides.

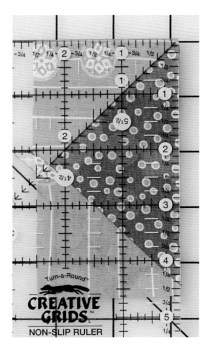

9. Rotate the block to trim the remaining sides. You won't be able to use the 45° angle, so line up the point at the ¼″ mark on your ruler, with the trimmed edges aligned at the 2½″ and 4½″ ruler lines, to get a perfect Flying Geese block. Trim the block to 2½″ × 4½″.

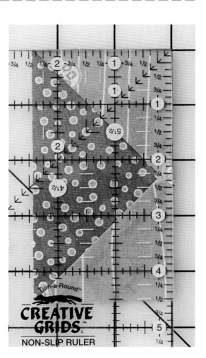

10. Repeat Steps 5–9 to create 2 more Flying Geese from the second heart shape.

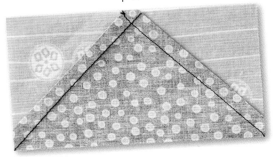

NOTE: From time to time when you make Flying Geese blocks, your block measurements may be off and you will have to make small adjustments as you trim. Instead of cutting off a point, shift your ruler up or down to ensure perfect points. Your block will be slightly larger or smaller, and you can ease in the seam when you sew pieces together (page 22).

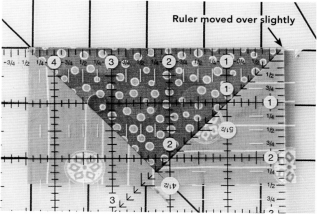

Move the ruler over slightly so you won't cut off the point.

FLYING GEESE VARIATION

If you don't like this method of making Flying Geese, you also can make them with two identical half-square triangles.

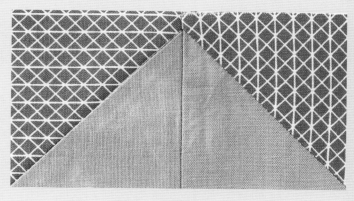

I like to press the center seam open if I make Flying Geese from half-square triangles.

CLASSIC FAVORITES

When I think about traditional quilts, these blocks come to mind. These blocks are some of the tried-and-true favorites for quilters. The blocks in this section represent a very small selection of classic favorites, but I think they clearly illustrate some common problems quilters have when making them. Several of the techniques in this section are new, and some are a combination of or variation on techniques discussed in the Building Blocks section (page 28).

Also included in this section are hints about how to dissect blocks differently. Many quilters are intimidated by a particular method, so I show you some alternative piecing options. Once you start to look at blocks differently, you can conquer some fears about more complex piecing.

52 Dutchman's Puzzle

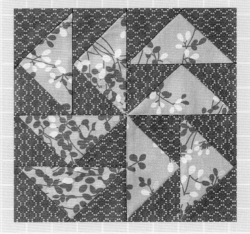

56 Square-in-a-Square

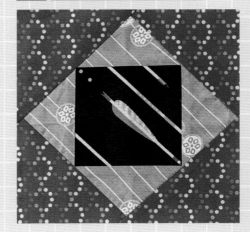

62 Log Cabin

66 Pinwheel

68 Sawtooth Star

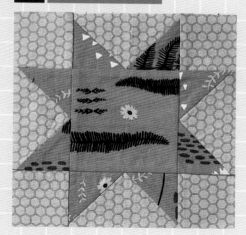

72 Ohio Star

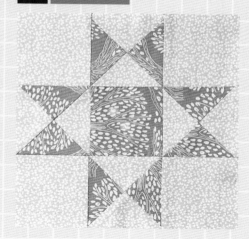

74 Ocean Waves

78 LeMoyne Star

Dutchman's PUZZLE

Problem ▶ Points will get cut off in the seam allowance, there is bulk at the center, and there are folds in the block when I press it.

What you don't want:

This point will get cut off in the seam allowance.

Improper pressing of the seam caused a fold.

How your block should look:

DIAGNOSIS

It's very easy to chop off a point in a Dutchman's Puzzle block if the Flying Geese units aren't put together correctly. Not furling seams in the center of the block will result in bulk and can cause you to press a fold in a seamline.

A Dutchman's Puzzle block is made of eight Flying Geese units sewn in pairs that rotate every quarter, creating a pinwheel in the center. If your Flying Geese are properly pieced, you should be able to avoid chopping off points. When you pin the blocks together, insert the pins ¼″ from the block edge to mark the seam allowance so you can watch the point placement as you stitch. Furling the back of the block will eliminate bulk in the center of the block and keep you from pressing a fold somewhere in the block.

1. Refer to the instructions in Flying Geese (page 46) to make 8 Flying Geese units. You will need to start with 2 large squares and 8 small squares. To determine the cutting size for the large squares, divide the finished size of the Dutchman's Puzzle block in half, and then add 1½″. To determine the cutting size for the small squares, divide the finished size of the Dutchman's Puzzle block by 4, and add 1″.

2. Sew the Flying Geese units together in sets of 2. If your Flying Geese units are not exactly the same size, gently ease in the excess (page 22) of the larger unit. Sew with the point of a Flying Geese unit on top so you can make sure you don't cut off the point. Press the seam allowance toward the top block.

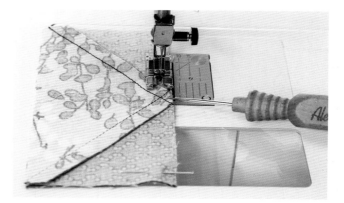

Tip Keep a tool nearby to help hold pieces that may get stuck in the needle or under your presser foot. While I really like Alex Anderson's 4-in-1 Essential Sewing Tool, I also have a precision screwdriver with a very small, flat head. The screwdriver doubles as a stiletto or pointer to help guide fabric through my machine. If a new tool isn't in your budget and you already own a small screwdriver, give it a try before making a purchase!

3. Arrange the Flying Geese units, rotating the direction of each pair so they appear to spin around the center. Sew the units together in pairs to make 2 half-blocks.

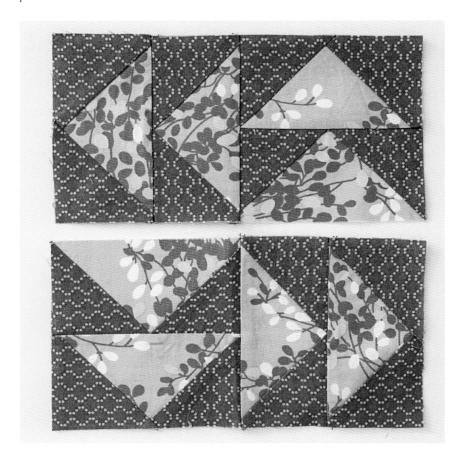

4. Place the block halves right sides together. Pin together, using the pin to mark each point. Sew the halves together.

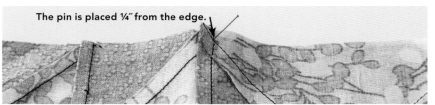

The pin is placed ¼˝ from the edge.

5. Furl the center seam allowance on the back of the block (page 27).

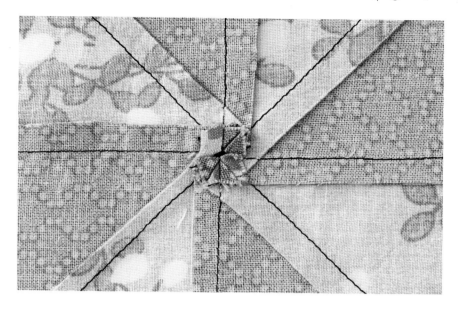

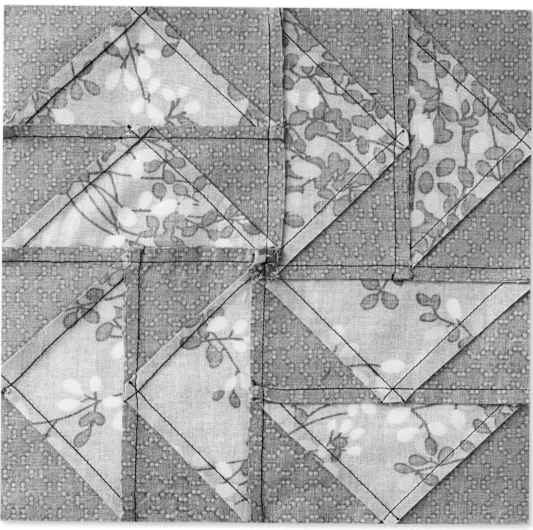

Square-
IN-A-
Square

Problem My block is not the correct size, a corner of the inside square has been chopped off, and my seam allowances are too small.

What you don't want:

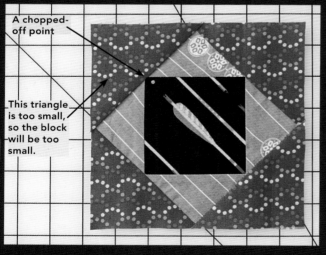

A chopped-off point

This triangle is too small, so the block will be too small.

How your block should look:

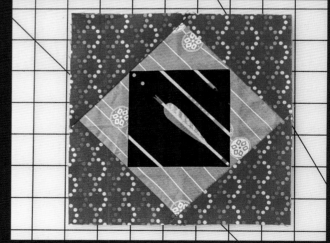

DIAGNOSIS

Cutting triangles too small and forcing them to fit will result in blocks that are too small, wavy edges or seams, and chopped-off points.

Determine correct sizes for triangles using a simple math formula, and trim to perfection.

The Square-in-a-Square block is one of my favorites! It's easy, you can make it any size you need to fit in your quilt, and you can show off special fabric by fussy cutting the square in the center. Square-in-a-Square makes a great center for other blocks, too!

There are multiple ways to make this block. You can paper piece, sew with squares, or cut four triangles and sew along the bias. I usually don't recommend sewing along the bias if it can be avoided, but it's my preferred method for this block. To avoid problems, cut the triangles larger than necessary and trim them down so your block is the right size and you won't cut off points.

I was intimidated by this block for a long time. I didn't know the math and came up with the most bizarre ways to get my blocks to finish at the size I wanted. I wasted a lot of fabric and a lot of energy getting frustrated. One day, however, a light went off in my head. A Square-in-a-Square block is basically two Flying Geese units put together. Just as I added half-square triangles to create the Flying Geese (page 46), I need to add half-

square triangles around the center square. Another step was realizing that for Square-in-a-Square blocks with two sets of triangles, the center square finishes exactly half the size of the finished block. So if I want a 6″ finished block I begin with a 3″ finished center. That's easy enough, right? Well, kind of. I still needed to know the size of the squares to make the triangles. That got easier when I realized there was a math formula to calculate the short sides of a triangle if I know the long side.

To find the size of the squares to cut for the center and the first set of triangles, use these formulas:

- finished block size ÷ 2 = finished center square

- finished center square + ½″ seam allowance = cut size of center square

- finished center square ÷ 1.414 = finished size of half-square triangle

- finished size of half-square triangle + 1″ + ½″ = cut size of squares for first set of triangles

I added 1″ to make Half-Square Triangles (page 38), and I recommend the extra ½″ so you know the triangles won't be too small. Also, the extra fabric will

give you plenty of leeway to trim and get a perfect block.

I will use a 5″ finished block as an example.

- 5″ ÷ 2 = 2½″, finished center square

- 2½″ + ½″ = 3″, cut size of center square

- 2½″ ÷ 1.414 = 1.768″, finished size of the half-square triangle. Round this to 1¾″.

- 1¾″ + 1″ + ½″ = 3¼″, cut size of squares for first set of triangles

I rounded the finished size of the half-square triangle to 1¾″ since it was so close. I like to add the final ½″ for safety and accuracy, so these squares need to be 3¼″. Cut two squares for each block, and cut them in half diagonally to yield four triangles.

1. Place a triangle on 2 opposite sides of the center, right sides together. Make sure the points are approximately in the center. You will trim these down after the block is complete, so you don't have to be perfect, but close is better.

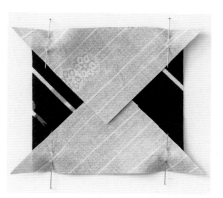

2. Sew the triangles to the square, taking care not to stretch the bias edges of the triangles as you sew. Set the seams and press the seam allowances away from the center square.

3. Sew a triangle to the other 2 sides of the center square.

4. Set the seams and press the seam allowances away from the center square.

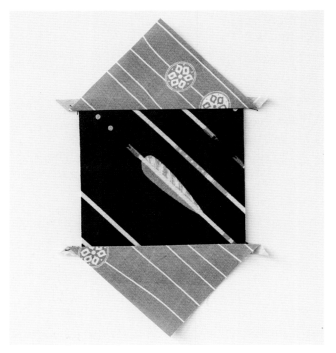

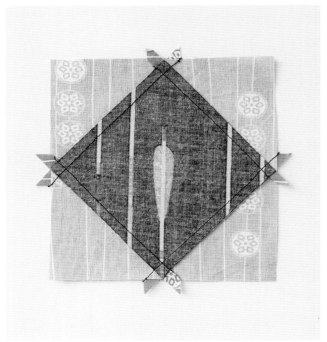

5. Trim the square. Square up the first side by aligning a horizontal line on the ruler with the diagonal of the square. Trim the little bit of excess on the right.

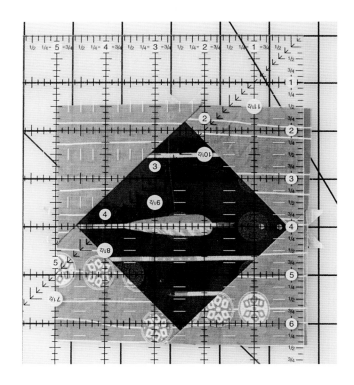

6. Rotate the block so the cut side is at the bottom. Align a horizontal line on the ruler with the bottom of the block. Along the right-hand side, align the ¼″ vertical line with the point of the center square. Trim the excess.

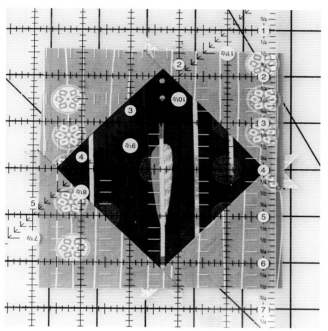

Align a horizontal line on the ruler across the center square.

7. Repeat the process to trim the remaining sides, including the first edge that you squared up.

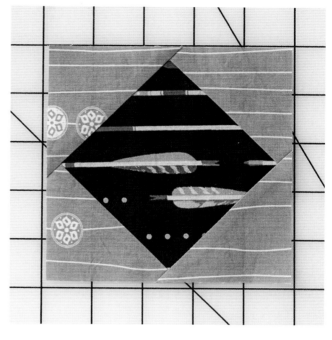

8. To find what size squares to cut for the second set of triangles, use the block center from Step 7 and follow the same technique used for the first set:

- finished size of block from Step 7 ÷ 1.414 = finished size of half-square triangle

- finished size of half-square triangle + 1″ = cut size of squares for second set of triangles

My rule of thumb for the second set of triangles is to use the finished size of the half-square triangle + 1″. I'm never short, and it's faster math. Cut 2 squares, and cut each square in half diagonally to yield 4 triangles.

9. Pin a triangle to 2 opposite sides of the pieced center. Try to center the triangles as much as possible.

10. Sew with the center block on top so you can see as you sew and avoid chopping off points. Set the seams and press the seam allowances toward the outer triangles.

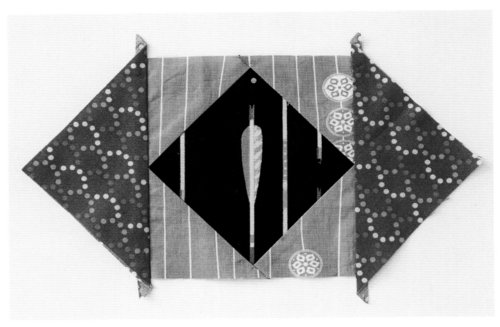

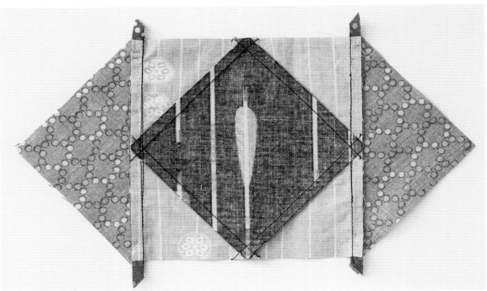

11. Sew a triangle to the remaining 2 sides of the center. Set seams and press toward the outer triangles.

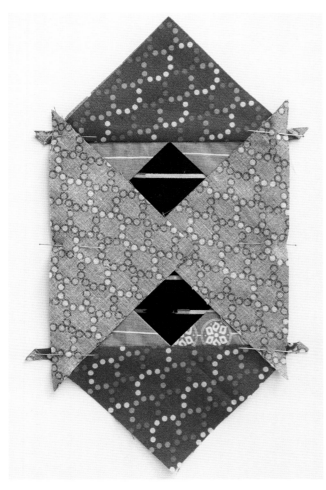

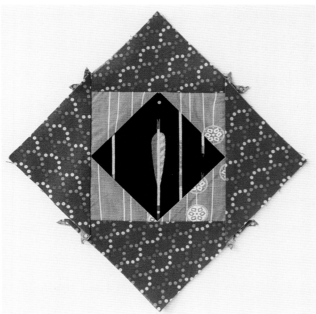

12. Trim the block, using the process shown in Steps 5–7.

Tip **More Math**

Another way to find the size of the setting triangles is to use half the diagonal of the center square. It gives you the same measurement and you don't need to remember 1.414. This is helpful if you know the size of the center square (rather than the finished block) and you want to make setting triangles that will fit. For example, if you fussy cut the center squares for your quilt blocks a certain size, you can find what size setting triangles will fit:

Diagonal of finished center square ÷ 2 = finished size of half-square triangles

Finished size of half-square triangles + 1″ = cut size of squares

You may want to add another ½″ for safety. Cut two squares, and cut each in half diagonally to yield four triangles.

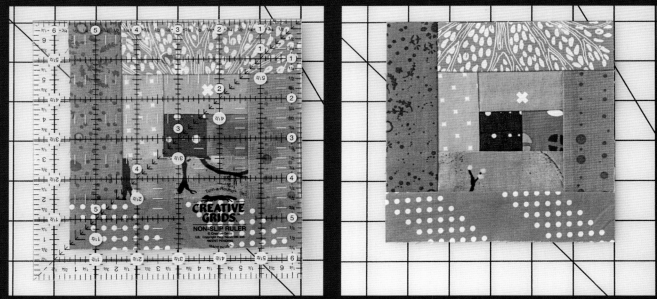

This block should finish at 5½˝. It is almost ¼˝ larger in some places.

You didn't square the blocks while sewing, or your ¼˝ seam isn't accurate.

The Log Cabin block is a favorite for quilters. The blocks are easy to make and a great way to use scraps. In addition, the blocks can be arranged in a wide variety of settings to make interesting quilts. To make your blocks finish at the correct size, an accurate ¼″ seam is crucial. A ¼″ variance on each of seven blocks means your quilt size can be off by 1¾″. That's a lot!

Make sure you square up your block as you go. Trimming the tiniest bit of fabric can be the difference between perfect blocks and blocks that don't finish at the size you want. It is particularly important that the first few units be perfectly square. If they aren't, not only can your block finish at an incorrect size, it can finish out of square.

I like to assembly-line piece my Log Cabin blocks if I am using the same fabrics in each block. It is much faster than cutting each strip (log) to size. However, Log Cabin blocks are great for scrap quilts. If you make blocks from scraps, cut your pieces slightly longer than the strip you need, if you can, so you can easily square up after pressing.

These instructions are for Log Cabins that use the same fabrics in each block.

1. Cut the center squares and a strip that is the width of the first adjoining log. If you are making many of the same Log Cabin blocks, cut all of your centers and strips.

2. Sew the center blocks to the first strip of the Log Cabin block in assembly-line fashion.

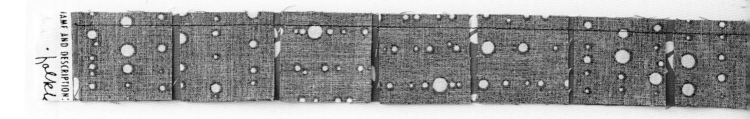

3. Cut the units apart. Set the seams and press the seam allowances toward the darker fabric.

4. Square up the unit.

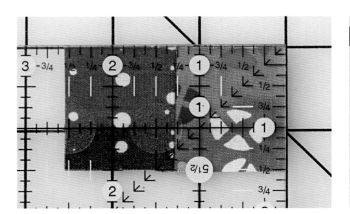

Tip If you piece your blocks from rectangular strips you have on hand or from scraps, cut the strips slightly longer than the specified cut size. It's easier to square up your block if you have some extra fabric!

5. Cut a strip the width of the next log and piece the units from Step 4 to it in assembly-line fashion.

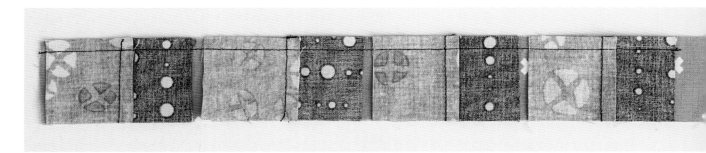

6. Cut the units apart. Set the seams, press the seam allowances to the side, and square up the units.

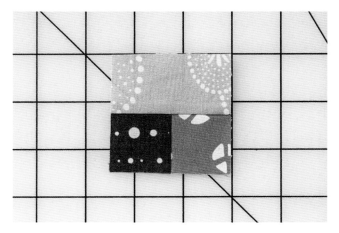

7. In the same manner, continue to add logs until you have completed the block. Square up the units after you add each log.

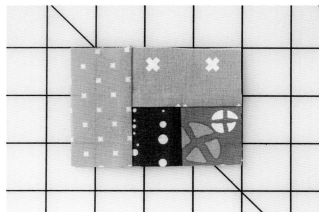

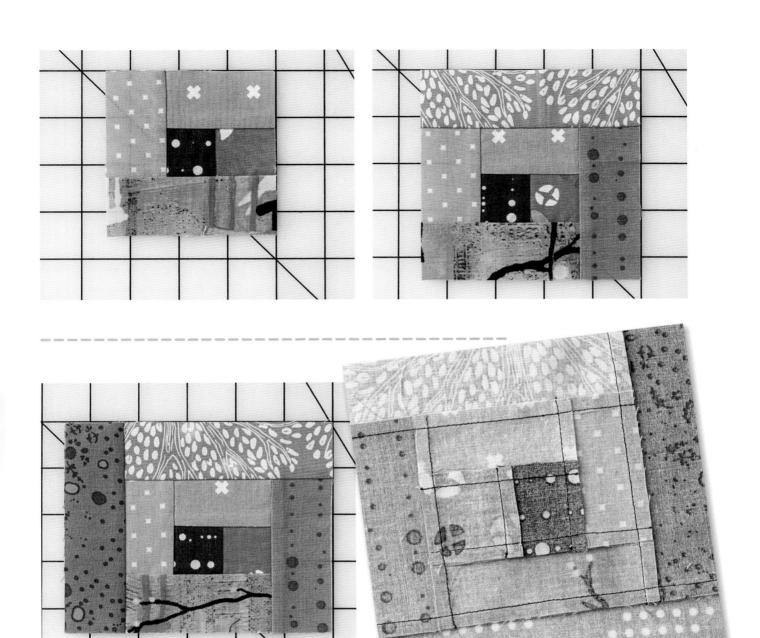

Tip If you followed all the rules and still have Log Cabin blocks that aren't the same size, consider adding coping strips (page 120).

Pinwheel

Problem → I've chopped off a point at the center, and there is bulk in the center of the block.

What you don't want: **How your block should look:**

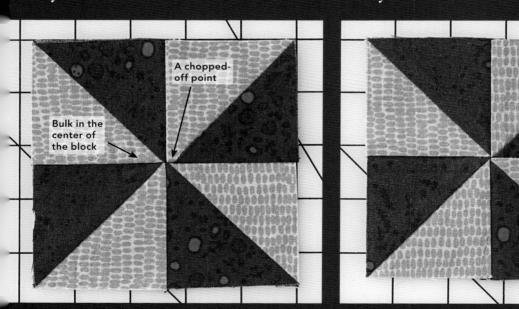

A chopped-off point

Bulk in the center of the block

DIAGNOSIS

If you don't start with accurate half-square triangle units, you can chop off a point. Not furling the center seams on the back of your block will result in bulk.

Pinwheel blocks are so much fun, but making them takes a little finesse. Perfect Half-Square Triangles help (page 38), and so will using a pin exactly through the center of the block to make sure all the points match.

You can make Pinwheels any size! Once you determine the finished size you need, divide that in half to determine the finished size of the half-square triangles.

1. Start with 4 half-square triangles. Arrange the half-square triangles to rotate around the center of the block, with points meeting at the center. Sew 2 half-square triangles together, making sure that the seams nest before you stitch (page 21).

2. Set the seams and press the seam allowances in opposite directions.

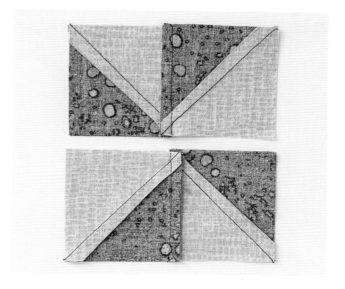

3. Lay the units right sides together, matching the center seam. Place a straight pin through the point in each block.

4. Stitch the units together. Carefully remove a few of the vertical and diagonal stitches at the center seam so you can furl the seam allowance.

5. Set the seam, and then finger-press the seams open at the intersection to make a small pinwheel. Press the seam allowances in opposite directions.

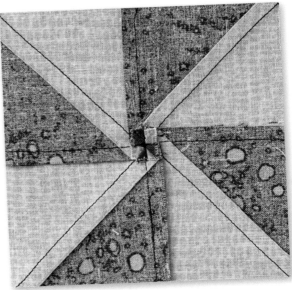

Sawtooth
STAR

Problem → I've cut off the point on one of my Flying Geese units, and my block is nowhere near square.

What you don't want:

How your block should look

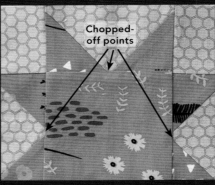

The block's not close to square.

Chopped-off points

This block is too small in places on each side and ¼″ short at the top.

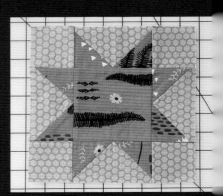

DIAGNOSIS

If your Flying Geese units aren't perfect, you will cut off a point. You can ease in seams to make the block units fit together, but if you overdo it, your blocks won't finish anywhere close to square.

SOLUTION

I tell students to think of a Sawtooth Star as a big, modified Nine-Patch block. If you have seams that don't nest, you can ease them in (page 22) so everything matches. Flying Geese units that aren't perfect will cause this block to be off, so perfecting those units (page 46) is the key to making a great Sawtooth Star block.

Over the years I've heard more than a few grumbles about this block. Most of them are from newer quilters who absolutely hate Flying Geese units. While I like to think that quilters will outgrow their disdain for Flying Geese, that's not always the case. If you hate making Flying Geese, see Flying Geese Variation (page 49) to make them with half-square triangles instead.

1. To make this block, start with 4 Flying Geese units, 1 large center square, and 4 corner squares.

- The finished size of the center square should be half the finished size of the Sawtooth Star block.

- The finished size of the Flying Geese will be the width of the center square × half the height of the center square.

- The finished size of the corner squares will be the same as the height of the Flying Geese.

Front before piecing

2. Sew the units into 3 rows.

Tip When I can, I sew with the Flying Geese unit on top so I can see the point and adjust my seam accordingly. I like to use a stiletto or other pointed object to keep the fabric bulk from getting caught in my needle.

3. Set the seams, and press the seam allowances of the Flying Geese in the middle row toward the center square. This will reduce bulk.

4. Pin 2 rows together. Make sure you nest the seams together (page 21) and piece with the Flying Geese unit on top. Set the seam and press.

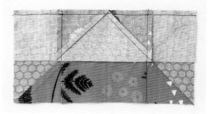

5. Sew the last row to the block. Set the seam and press.

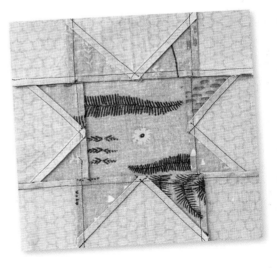

SAWTOOTH STAR VARIATIONS

If you don't like to make Flying Geese, you can substitute Half-Square Triangles.

Press the half-square triangles open to reduce bulk in the seams.

The back of your block will look like this when you have it sewn together.

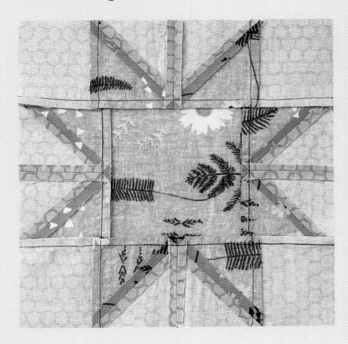

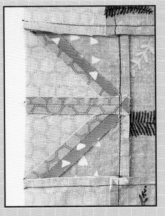

Tip Try to sew with the triangle units on top. This allows you to see where the point is and not chop it off. Remember, you want to sew a thread or two above the point so the block is perfect when you press. Occasionally, if you don't sew close enough to the point, you can just sew the seam again and try to get closer to the point. Usually I recommend you take out the stitches and sew again. However, in this case, since the seam allowance is pressed into the center of the block, that's unnecessary work. An extra row of stitches won't make a difference or increase bulk when the block is finished.

A Sawtooth Star with a Square-in-a-Square block in the center

The Sawtooth Star is a perennial favorite for quilters because of its versatility. It's ideal for scrap quilts because there are so many variations. You can make it with the center as a single piece of fabric, with different blocks in the center, with half-square triangles, with scrappy points, or with scrappy centers. The possibilities are endless. Here are a few examples.

Different blocks in the center

A scrappy block made with half-square triangles

Ohio STAR

Problem → My points don't match, there is bulk in my seam, and I have less than a ¼″ seam allowance along some edges.

What you don't want:

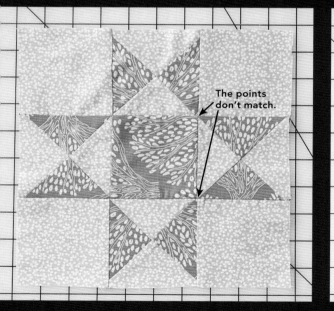

The points don't match.

How your block should look:

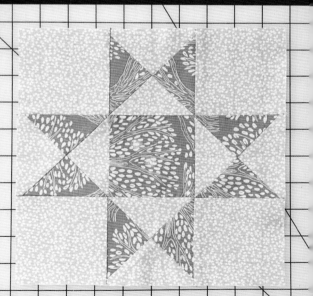

DIAGNOSIS

Make sure you have the correct seam allowance on your Quarter-Square Triangles (page 40) or you will chop off a point. Improperly pressing seams will result in bulk at the intersections of your pieces.

The Ohio Star block is a quilter's favorite, but it is easy to end up with more than a few chopped-off points and bulky seams. I know I've made my fair share! Matching points that are placed diagonally from one another should be easy, but even seasoned quilters can struggle and inadvertently chop one off here and there.

Nested seams and furled intersections will help you make your block as flat as possible. Make sure the quarter-square triangle units are square, and use a pin to help match points. If you cut and pieced your quarter-square triangle blocks correctly but still have a gap, ease in the seam (page 22) or carefully sew a seam that is just larger than a scant ¼˝.

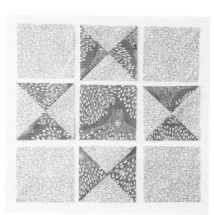

1. To make this block, start with a center square, 4 quarter-square triangles, and 4 corner squares. The finished size of each square and quarter-square triangle should be ⅓ of the finished Ohio Star block size.

2. Sew the units into 3 rows.

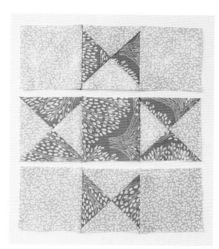

3. Set the seams and press the seam allowances toward the plain squares.

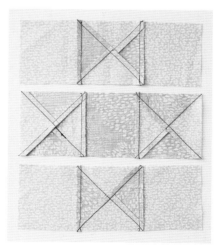

4. Pin 2 rows right sides together. Use a pin to match each of the 2 points.

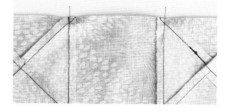

5. Sew the 2 rows together. Set the seam.

6. Sew the remaining row to the block.

7. Carefully remove a few stitches from the seam allowances at the corners of the center square so you can furl the seam allowances (page 27).

8. Set the seam, and then finger-press the seam open at the intersections to make small pinwheels. Press the seam allowances in opposite directions.

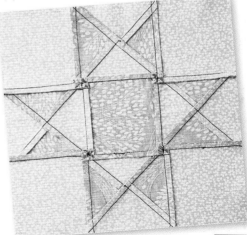

Ocean
WAVES

Problem Points don't match, the seams are bulky, and there is a wave in the block.

What you don't want:

How your block should look

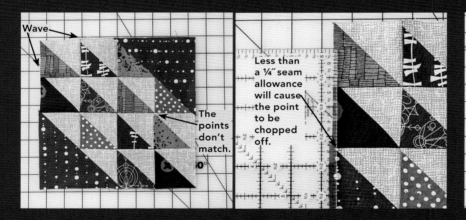

Wave

The points don't match.

Less than a ¼″ seam allowance will cause the point to be chopped off.

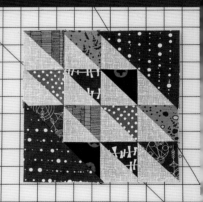

DIAGNOSIS

Not pressing the seams open on an Ocean Waves block will result in points that don't match, a wave in your block, and bulk at the seam intersections.

Ocean Waves is a serious block. It looks easy enough with a bunch of half-square triangles, but don't let that fool you. There are so many intersections that this block is not for the faint of heart! But the effort is worth it; this block is gorgeous when finished!

The biggest key to making a successful Ocean Waves block is pressing the seams open on the half-square triangles. In Half-Square Triangle (page 38), I discuss why some half-square triangles should be pressed open while others should be pressed to one side. If you are matching a lot of points, as in Ocean Waves, you are almost always better off pressing the seams open. In addition to reducing bulk, pressing the seams open makes it easier to see where the points are when you sew the squares together.

1. To make this block, start with 10 half-square triangles, 4 small triangles (2 light and 2 dark), and 2 large triangles.

- The finished size of the half-square triangles should be ¼ of the finished size of the Ocean Waves block. Press the seams of the half-square triangles open.

- To cut the large triangles, start with a square that is ½ the finished size of the Ocean Waves block, plus 1˝. Cut it in half diagonally to yield 2 triangles.

- To cut the small triangles, start with a light square and a dark square that are ¼ the finished size of the Ocean Waves block, plus 1˝. Cut each square in half to yield 2 triangles.

For this example I am making an 8˝ finished block, so the half-square triangles are 2˝ finished. The small triangles were cut from 3˝ squares, and the large triangles were cut from a 5˝ square.

2. Sew the half-square triangles and triangles into 4 rows. Set the seams and press the seam allowances open.

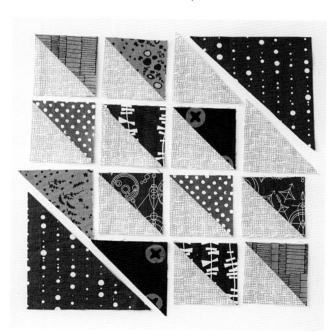

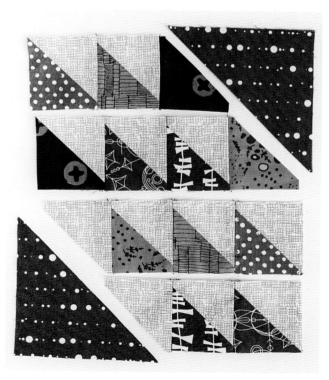

3. Pin 2 rows together. Use a pin to mark the points on each side.

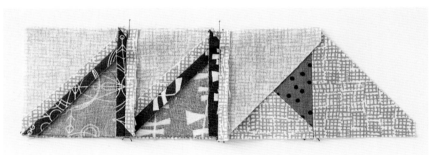

4. Sew the rows together, taking care not to cut off a point. Set the seam and press the seam allowances open.

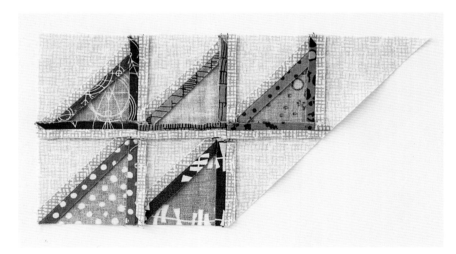

5. Repeat Steps 3 and 4 to sew together the remaining 2 rows.

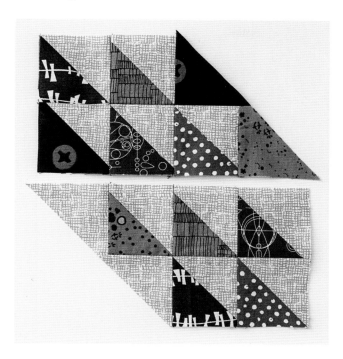

6. Sew the 2 sections together. Mark the points and watch them as you sew so you don't cut them off. Set the seam and press the seam allowance open.

7. Sew a large triangle to each side of the block. Remember that you will have bunny ears, or small triangles, hanging off the sides.

8. Set the seams and press toward the large triangle.

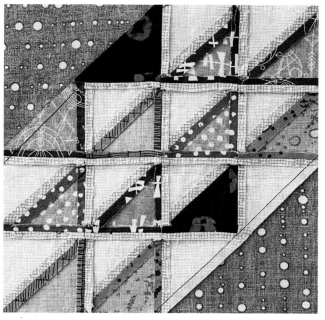

NOTE: It seems weird to press the last two seams to one side, since all the other seams are pressed open. But pressing open the last two seams will create bulk at the points of the small triangles.

LeMoyne STAR

Problem → My block has wave, there is bulk in the center, and my Y-seams don't match.

What you don't want:

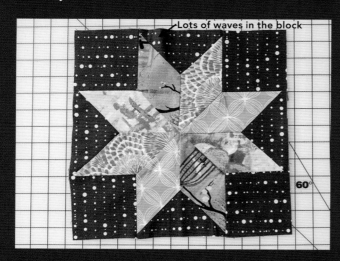

Lots of waves in the block

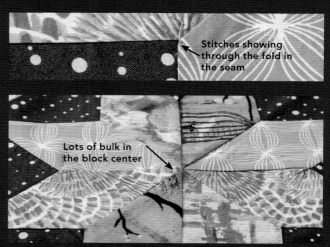

Stitches showing through the fold in the seam

Lots of bulk in the block center

60°

How your block should look:

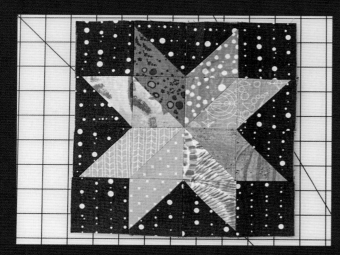

60°

The sides of LeMoyne Star diamonds are on the bias. If you stretch them while piecing, you will create wave in your block. The bulk in the center of the block is the result of improper piecing and pressing.

------------------------------ **SOLUTION** ------------------------------

Piecing a LeMoyne Star block using diamond-shaped pieces can create a myriad of problems: waves, bulky centers, and Y-seams that don't match. While I love the look of this block when it's pieced with diamonds, it can be intimidating for anyone who has not mastered a Y-seam.

This method is an easy way to modify a LeMoyne Star by using Half-Square Triangles (page 38) instead of diamonds. You can make the blocks any size you want, you don't have to wrangle pattern pieces for the diamonds, and you don't have to sew any Y-seams.

Tip Pay attention to your fabric choices if you make a LeMoyne Star using half-square triangle units. Smaller prints work better because their patterns will blend across the seamline, making it look as if you used a single diamond. Make sure you mix and match the fabrics so your block will have more interest.

Front before piecing

1. To make this block, start with 4 half-square triangles for the center using a combination of all the fabrics, 8 half-square triangles for the outer edges combining each star fabric with the background fabric, and 4 corner squares. Be sure to press the half-square triangle seams open to reduce bulk.

- The finished size of each half-square triangle and each corner square should be ¼ of the finished size of the LeMoyne Star block.

Tip Since you can make two identical half-square triangles from a pair of squares, you will end up with twice as many half-square triangles as you need for a LeMoyne Star. It will be tempting to use both half-square triangles in your block. If you do, plan the placement so they are diagonally opposite

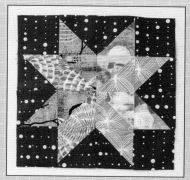

Placing the same fabrics in adjacent triangles can make your block look lopsided.

each other. If you use identical triangles on adjacent sides of the star, your block will look lopsided.

As an alternative, make two LeMoyne Star blocks to use up all your half-square triangles, or save the extras for another project.

2. Sew the units into 4 rows. Set the seams and press the seam allowances open.

Tip If you are worried about matching points, measure ¼″ from the edge of the unit to find the point along the diagonal seam on each block. Stick a pin through that mark.

3. Sew 2 rows together to make a half-block. Use pins to mark the points. Set the seams and press open.

4. Sew the 2 halves together. Mark the points with a pin so you don't chop any off.

Tip A LeMoyne Star made with half-square triangles is similar to a Sawtooth Star (page 68). You can make a LeMoyne Star block in the same way you make a Sawtooth Star block by using Flying Geese on the outside edges instead of half-square triangles.

5. Set the seams and press them open.

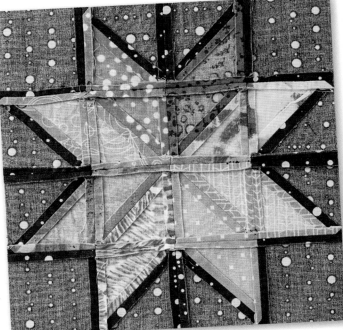

LEMOYNE STAR MADE WITH DIAMONDS

The LeMoyne Star is a beautiful block when it's pieced with diamonds.

There are a few tricks to making this block cooperate with you. Press all the seams in one direction.

Press the Y-seams into the diamonds to make them lie flat.

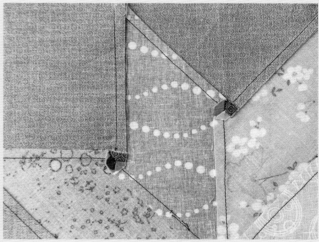

To piece the block with Y-seams, start by marking the points of the diamonds where the ¼˝ seam allowances would intersect. Stitch the diamonds together in sets of four, starting and stopping at each point to leave the seam allowance unsewn. Backstitch at each end of the seams, taking care not to stitch into the seam allowance. When you piece the two halves of the block together, sew just above the marked points. The center will furl into a star, making it lie flat.

MODERN FAVORITES

The blocks and techniques in this section come to mind when
I think about modern favorites. Just like the Classic Favorites
section, this is a small sampling, but I see these frequently. Most of
these blocks are classic favorites that have been brought back to life
by the modern quilt movement. The size, scale, and fabric choices
of the following blocks lend themselves to some very cool quilts.
While any block can be made modern, these truly shine.

84 Blocks with Narrow Accent Strips

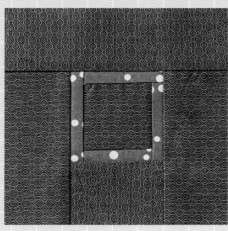

86 Drunkard's Path

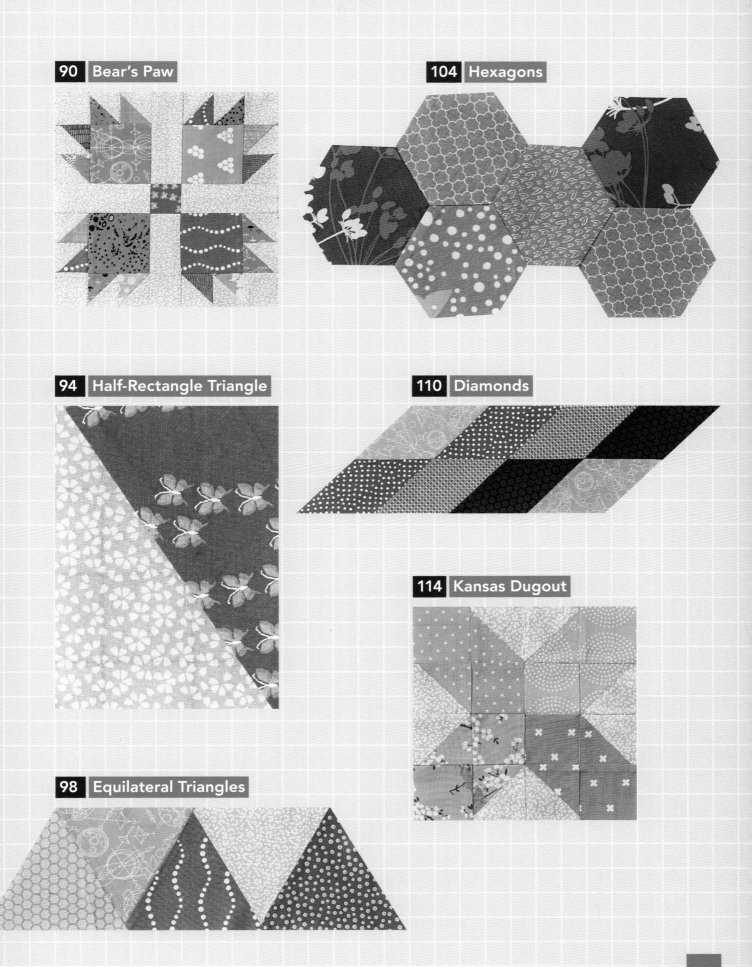

90 Bear's Paw

104 Hexagons

94 Half-Rectangle Triangle

110 Diamonds

114 Kansas Dugout

98 Equilateral Triangles

Blocks WITH Narrow Accent Strips

Problem ▸ My narrow strips are uneven and my block isn't square.

What you don't want:

How your block should look:

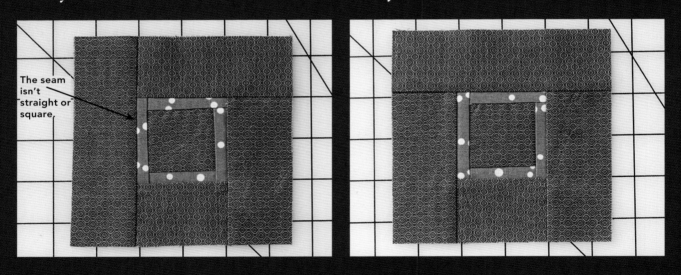

The seam isn't straight or square.

DIAGNOSIS

Sewing narrow strips requires patience and precision. If you are the slightest bit off when you sew, you will have a less-than-perfect seam. It can be a challenge even for experienced quilters.

SOLUTION

Piecing a block with narrow strips seems like it would be easy. You sew a straight line, you get a narrow strip. Right? Wrong. I remember the first time I made a quilt with a ¼″ accent in the border. Let's just say my narrow border wasn't exactly straight. The smallest bit of drag on the pieces or just a little bit of human error can cause a narrow strip of fabric to get a bow. A small bow may not be noticeable in larger pieces of fabrics, but the same bow will show in small strips. Sometimes your seams are perfect but your eyes trick you into thinking your seam isn't straight. Get out a ruler and measure. Your ruler won't lie.

Starch is definitely your friend when you are sewing with narrow strips. The added stability helps prevent waves in your strip.

I have found I get better results if I replace a perfectly cut narrow strip with a piece that is oversized, so I can square up my block and trim it to the correct size. This method does waste some fabric and takes extra time, but the results are worth it.

Here is an example with a very simple block.

1. Sew oversized narrow strips to the center of the block. Set the seams and press toward the narrow strips as you sew.

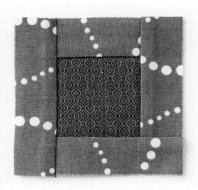

2. Place your ruler on the block. I plan to make finished ¼″ accent strips, so I aligned the ruler with the right and top seamlines at the ½″ mark to leave room for the finished ¼″ and the remaining ¼″ seam allowance. Be sure to align the ruler with the seamlines both horizontally and vertically so you keep the block square. Trim the first 2 sides.

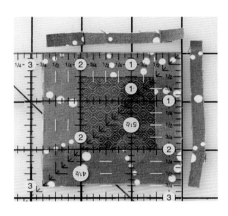

3. Rotate the block and trim the remaining 2 sides.

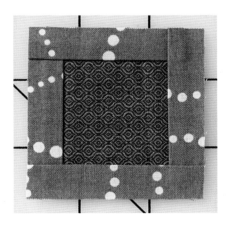

4. Sew the outer strips to your block, pressing toward the outer strip as you go. For this example, I used oversized strips on the outside edge so I could trim down the block.

Tip You will get a better result if you sew the pieces together with the narrow strip on top. It allows you to shift the fabric while piecing.

5. Trim the excess from each side, aligning the ruler markings with the seamlines to make sure you keep the block square.

Tip This is a great method to use for inner borders and accent pieces. Just remember to cut the strip wider than necessary and trim down.

Drunkard's

PATH

Problem → My pieces don't fit together.

What you don't want:

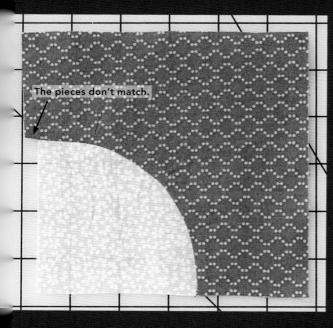

The pieces don't match.

How your block should look:

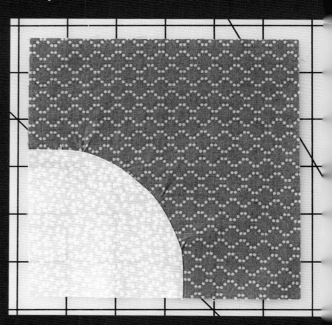

DIAGNOSIS

Sewing in an arc or a circle means the majority of the seam is sewn on the bias. If we know anything about bias, we know that it stretches. If you pull on either piece a little too much, or not enough, your block will

Well before I ever sewed a curved seam in a quilt block, I set in a lot of sleeves in clothing. Along the way, I occasionally had to redo a sleeve or two. Little did I know that all my practice would help me sew perfect curved seams in quilt blocks.

If you've ever sewn a curved block, you know it can be a little intimidating. The best piece of advice I can give you is to pin, pin, and pin! Especially if sewing a curve is new for you.

I've seen quilters use a variety of techniques to sew curved seams. I've tried a few different ones over the years and found what works best for me. I like to find the center and midpoints of each piece. Pin the ends and the center so you can ease in the excess, pinning along the way. If you haven't sewn with curved seams before, you cannot use too many pins.

1. To make this block, start with a block background and a quarter-circle arc.

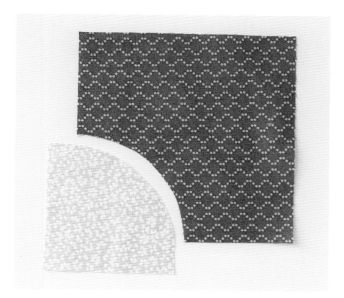

2. Fold the block background in half. Press with a pressing tool or your fingers. You don't need to press with an iron. You need just enough of a pressed line to align with the arc.

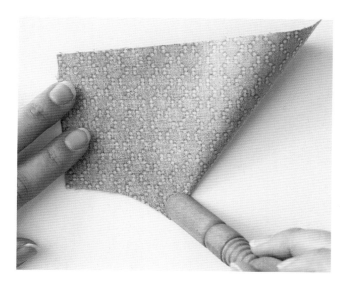

3. Fold each side in half again and press.

4. Fold the arc in half to mark the center.

5. Fold each side in half again and press.

Your pieces will look like you made paper accordions from them when you finish.

6. Right sides together, pin the centers of the pieces together.

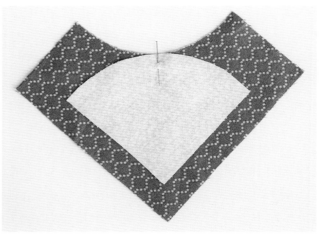

7. Pin the ends together, making sure the edges are parallel with each other.

8. Pin the rest of the seam, matching the fold marks you made. The larger piece of fabric will be bunched up. Don't worry. As long as the seam allowance is flat, your block will be fine.

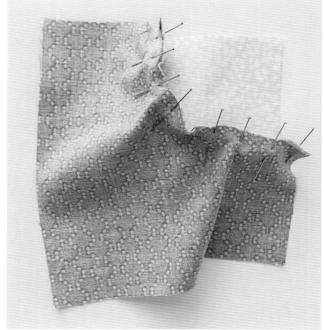

9. With the quarter-circle arc on the bottom, carefully sew the pieces together. Remove pins as you sew.

10. Set the seam. Press the seam allowance toward the arc, or as needed for your project so that seam allowances will nest.

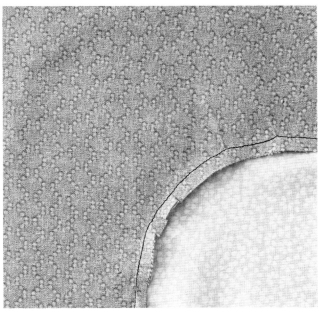

Tip Occasionally a curved seam has a spot here or there that needs a little help flattening out. If that happens, you don't have to take apart the block and sew it again. Using a small, sharp pair of scissors, carefully clip the curve, making sure you don't clip into the stitching. Clipping will relax the fabric and make imperfections less noticeable.

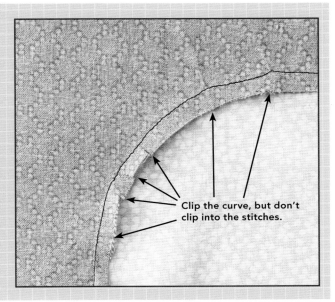

Clip the curve, but don't clip into the stitches.

Bear's PAW

Problem → The points on the outside edges of my block will get cut off in the seam allowance.

What you don't want:

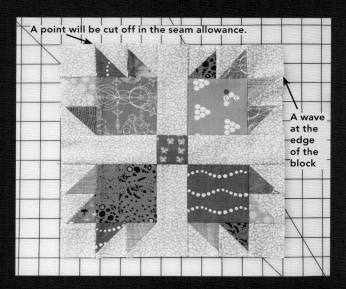

A point will be cut off in the seam allowance.

A wave at the edge of the block

How your block should look:

If you don't piece the half-square triangle units to the correct size, you risk cutting points off in the seam allowance. There are a lot of pieces in this block. Any distortion, incorrect seam allowances, or improper

Making a Bear's Paw block is an exercise in patience. The block looks easy enough, but if you are not careful when you piece the half-square triangles, or you are sloppy when you piece the block, you will end up chopping off a point. What makes this block even more challenging is the fact that each side has four points that need to match up with another block or sashing when you set the blocks together.

The Bear's Paw block is a great example of a block where you need to think about pressing smaller units before you piece the block. Not only do you need to think about pressing the half-square triangles, but you need to think about this block as a Nine-Patch (page 36) and make sure you press sections so you can easily piece blocks together or join the block to sashing.

The Bear's Paw block is unusual in that you can press your half-square triangles open or to one side and it doesn't make much difference in the overall appearance of the block. It is important to consider how you plan to sew the blocks into the quilt. If you plan to sew blocks together without sashing in between, press the half-square triangles open to avoid excessive bulk at the edges of the blocks. If you plan to use sashing, you can press the seams to one side or press them open. I like to press to one side and will show you that in this chapter.

1. For each quadrant of this block, you will need a large square, 4 half-square triangles, and a corner square. To piece the quadrants together, you will need a center square and 4 sashing rectangles. If you make the sashing rectangles the same width as the half-square triangles, then each element of the block is based on $1/7$ of the finished block size. So this is a good pattern for block sizes that are multiples of 7, like $3\frac{1}{2}''$, $7''$, $10\frac{1}{2}''$, $14''$, and so on.

- The finished size of the half-square triangles, the corner squares, and the center square will be $1/7$ of the finished size of the Bear's Paw block.

- The large square will be $2/7$ of the finished size of the Bear's Paw block.

- The width of the sashing rectangles will be the same as the width of the center square. The length should equal the length of a pieced quadrant.

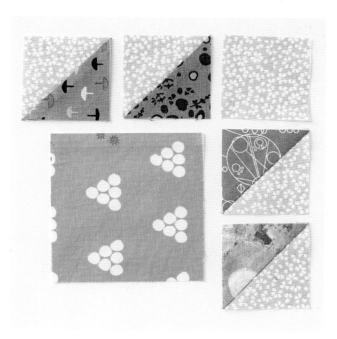

2. Sew each section of a quadrant together. Pay special attention to the orientation of the half-square triangles.

Front

3. Sew the first 2 sections together with the triangle units on top. You are less likely to chop off a point if you can see it. Use a stiletto or other tool to keep the seam allowances from getting caught under the needle in your machine. Set the seam, and press the seam allowance toward the large square.

4. Sew the remaining unit to the quadrant. Make sure you nest your seams together. Set the seams, and press the seam allowances toward the large square.

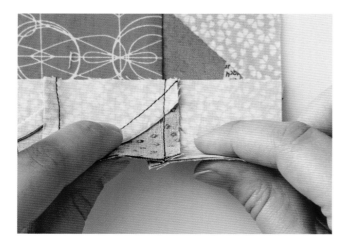

Make 4.

5. Arrange the block elements. The seams from the half-square triangle units press into the larger center square to reduce bulk.

6. Sew the units into 3 rows.

7. Press the seams between rows in opposite directions so they'll nest when you put them together.

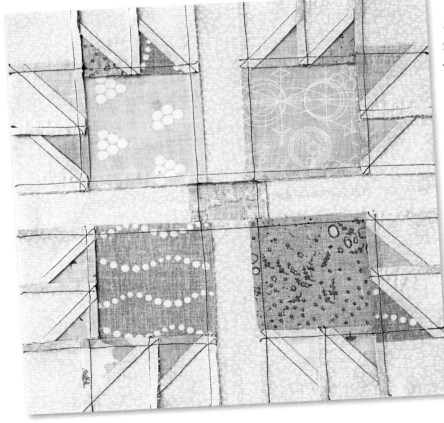

8. Sew the units together. Set the seams, and press the block.

Half-Rectangle
TRIANGLE

Problem → My Half-Rectangle Triangle units turned out completely wrong. My blocks have a curve or wave.

What you don't want:

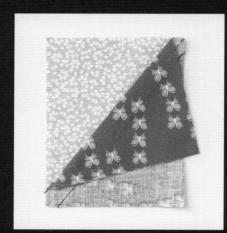

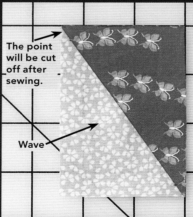

The point will be cut off after sewing.

Wave

How your block should look:

DIAGNOSIS

You cut or pieced your Half-Rectangle Triangle block incorrectly or you stretched the pieces while sewing, creating a curve.

I remember the first time I made a Half-Rectangle Triangle. I thought I could make the blocks just like a Half-Square Triangle but with rectangles. I was wrong and ended up with a kite. Definitely not what I wanted! As it turns out, there is a trick to making Half-Rectangle Triangles. I learned it quickly but was a little embarrassed by my mistake.

You may be tempted to add ⅞″ or 1″ to cut the rectangles, but the exact amount needed depends on the ratio of the width to the length. Generally, adding 1½″ to the length and 1½″ to the width will give you leeway to trim the block to size. If your ratio is very different, you may need to experiment first with scrap fabric.

There are two important rules to follow when making Half-Rectangle Triangles. The first is to mark the rectangle correctly, and the second is to shift the fabrics and sew with one piece at a slight angle to the other. Unlike Half-Square Triangles that are marked from corner to corner, these rectangles are marked ½″ from the corners with the marks going in the same direction. The fabric will then be shifted when the pieces are placed right sides together. For this example, I am making a 2″ × 3″ finished Half-Rectangle Triangle.

1. Cut 2 rectangles 1½″ longer and 1½″ wider than the finished size. We'll use 2 rectangles 3½″ × 4½″, which will finish as 2″ × 3″ Half-Rectangle Triangles.

2. On the front of each rectangle, use the marking tool of your choice to place a corner dot exactly ½″ from the edge. Draw a second dot on the corner diagonally opposite the first.

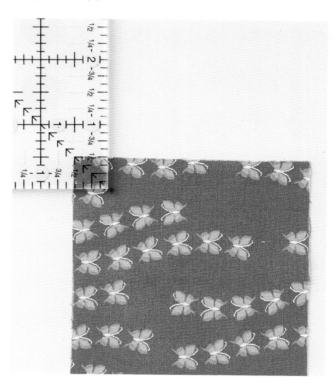

3. On the wrong side, draw a line between the 2 dots. Make sure the diagonal lines are angled in the same direction on both rectangles.

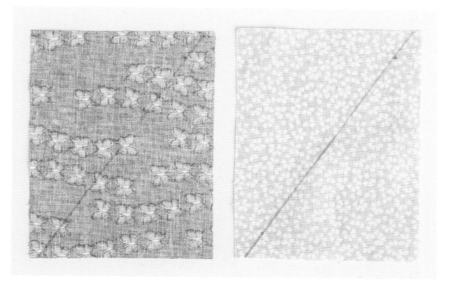

4. Place the rectangles right sides together, matching the dots, with the diagonal lines aligned.

5. Place a pin through each of the ½" marks.

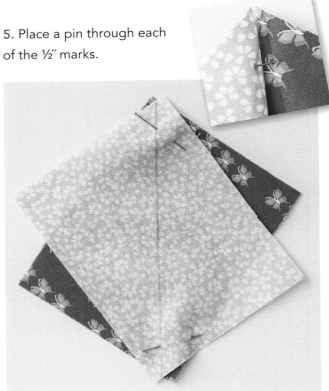

6. Sew ¼" from each side of the diagonal line. Set the seam, and then cut along the marked line.

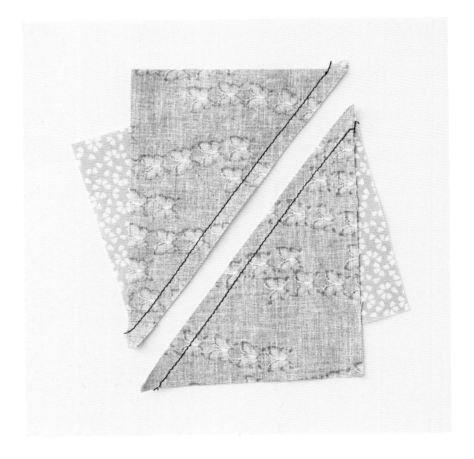

7. Press the seam open or to the side, depending on how you plan to use the block.

8. Square up your block. Line up each corner with the appropriate measurement to trim, placing the point where the 2 colors meet ¼″ in from the edges. I am making a 2″ × 3″ rectangle, so the corners of my cut rectangle will be at 2½″ and 3½″ on the ruler.

NOTE: Remember that the diagonal of your rectangle isn't at a 45° angle. Pay attention to this when you trim and make sure you line up the ruler on your block correctly, taking your ¼″ seam allowance into account. It may be helpful to draw trim lines on your block so you don't make a mistake, or use a piece of paper that is the finished size of the rectangle. Your corners will look off, especially if you have a skinny rectangle. If your rectangles are very narrow or need to be perfectly pieced, paper piecing is a good option.

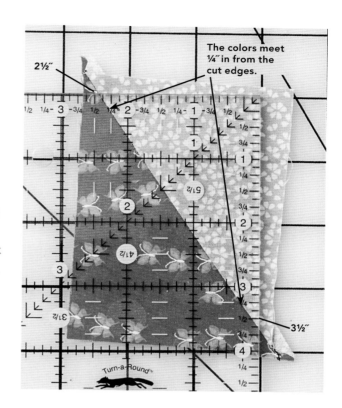

9. Rotate the block and trim the remaining sides.

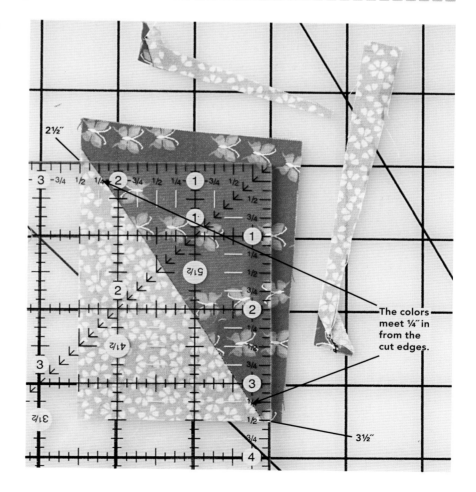

Equilatera

TRIANG

Problem ➤ My row of triangles isn't straight and it's wavy. Some of my seam allowances will finish at less than ¼″.

What you don't want:

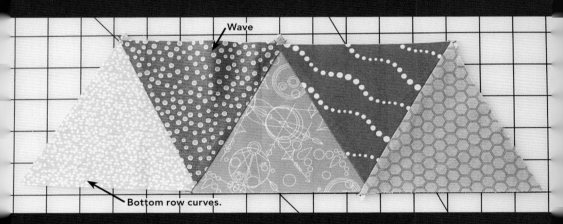

Wave

Bottom row curves.

How your blocks should look:

You stretched the pieces along the bias when sewing the triangles together and created a curve. Trying to straighten the curve results in a wave in your row. Pulling also can cause your seam allowance to be less than ¼˝.

━━━━━━━━━━━━━━━━━━━━━ **SOLUTION** ━━━━━━━━━━━━━━━━━━━━━

Equilateral Triangles are so easy and fun to piece, but you have to be careful not to stretch the pieces when you sew them together. Often that's easier said than done when you are sewing a row of bias edges together.

There are quite a few products that you can use to cut equilateral triangles. I prefer to cut strips and use the 60° guides on my ruler to cut triangles. When you cut triangles, make sure you stack your fabric with the grain going in one direction. That will help keep your quilt stable.

The key to sewing triangles together is to guide the fabric through the sewing machine gently. Don't pull the pieces; let the machine do all the work. Press the seams open. You could press the seams to one side, but then you would have to think about which way you press each row so you can nest the seams (page 21). I find it easier to press the seams open so I don't have to worry about it.

The formula for determining what size strip to use is easy. Add ¾˝ to the finished size (height) of the equilateral triangle. A 4¾˝ strip will be perfect for cutting 4˝ finished triangles.

1. Cut a strip of fabric. I cut a 4¾˝ strip to make 4˝ triangles.

2. Place the ruler so the 60° mark lines up with the bottom edge of the strip of fabric. I like to make the first cut just on the other side of the selvage so I have minimal waste.

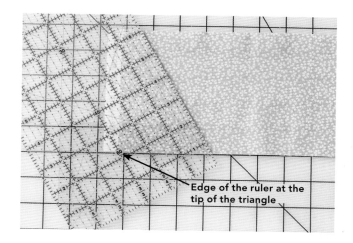

Edge of the ruler at the tip of the triangle

3. Cut off the edge (half an equilateral triangle is unused).

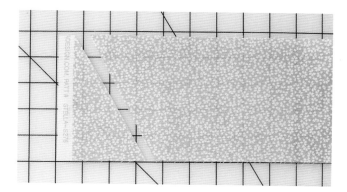

4. Reposition your ruler as shown, placing the 60° mark at the top edge of the strip. The ruler should meet the tip of the triangle at the bottom edge of the strip.

5. Continue to rotate the ruler or flip the strip to cut more triangles. Cut as many triangles as you need.

6. Place 2 triangles right sides together. An added bonus here is that you don't have to shift any pieces to allow for points!

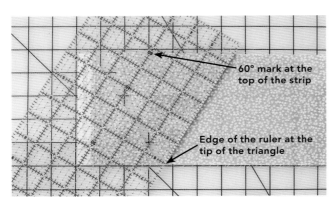

60° mark at the top of the strip

Edge of the ruler at the tip of the triangle

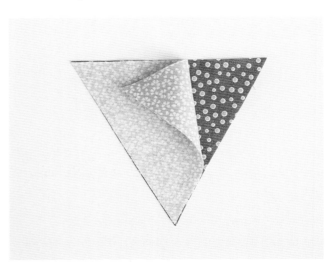

7. Sew the triangles together along an edge. Set the seam, and press the seam allowance open.

8. Place another triangle on the row of triangles, right sides together, and sew.

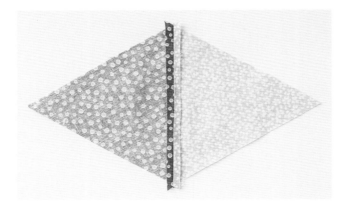

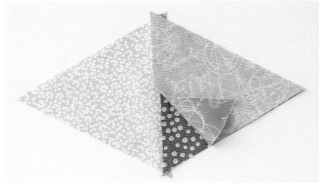

9. Set the seam, and press the seam allowance open.

10. Continue to sew triangles together until you reach your desired row length. Be sure to press seam allowances open as you go. For this example, each row has 5 triangles.

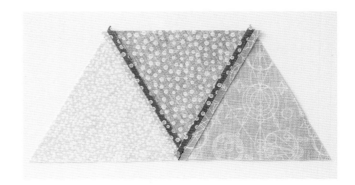

11. When you are ready to assemble the rows, place 2 rows right sides together. Put a pin through the points.

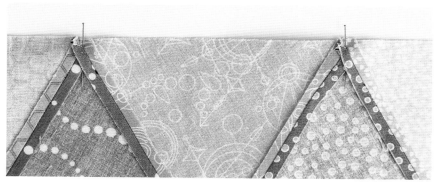

12. Sew the rows together. Set the seam and press the seam allowance open.

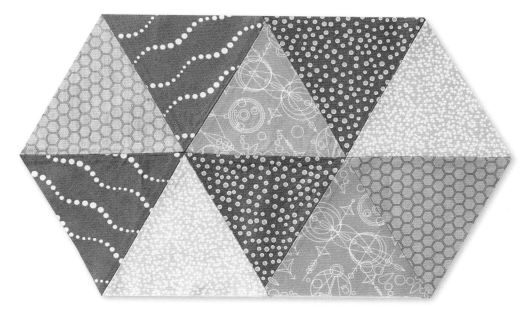

NOTE: When you sew the rows together, the pins will help keep the points matched up. Because the seams are pressed open, you can see where the points are and guide your needle to go just over them, in case you are slightly off on your ¼″ seam allowance.

CREATING HEXAGONS FROM TRIANGLES

You can use equilateral triangles to make hexagons. There are no Y-seams involved, and you can create great movement in your block!

Notice the difference in the three hexagons. The fabric for the light gray hexagon has a small overall print, and the seams are less noticeable.

The green fabric is directional. For this hexagon, all the waves are oriented in the same way. Using equilateral triangles to create depth and movement in hexagons can produce some wonderful effects. The small pink hexagon uses six different fabrics. This particular method is great for tessellation quilts and quilts with a lot of movement, where one piece of fabric blends with another.

You can press the backs of the hexagons in two different ways. You can press the seam allowances in one direction and furl the center (page 27).

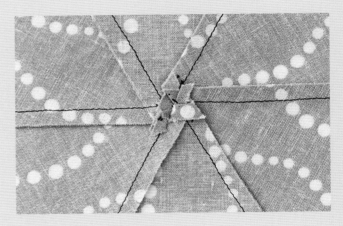

Or you can press the seams open, and then furl the center.

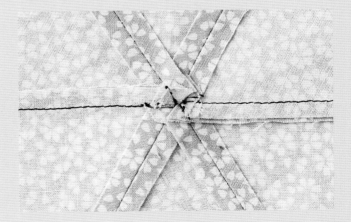

I don't think there is much difference as far as bulk at the intersection. I do, however, find it's easier to match the points if I press the seams open because I can see where the points are located.

Using Special Rulers If it's in your budget, there are some wonderful rulers for cutting equilateral triangles. You can use a 6″ × 24″ ruler, which most quilters have in their toolbox, but it's easier to cut correctly if you don't have to rotate the ruler constantly or try to match the 60° markings.

Equilateral triangle rulers come in a variety of sizes. Just like making an investment in square rulers, think about what sizes you make or think you'll make most often when you purchase a ruler. You can always cut a smaller triangle with a larger ruler, but you can't cut a larger triangle with a small ruler. On the other hand, large rulers can be bulky for cutting small pieces, so keep that in mind.

Personally, I find that the Clearview Triangle Super 60 (C&T Publishing) works well for most of my needs. I can cut 30°, 60°, and 120° angles, all using the same ruler. The ruler has clearly marked measurements and is easy to handle. There are rulers for cutting larger triangles and rulers with markings for cutting other shapes, like diamonds. Consider what shapes and sizes you use, or plan to use, and decide if a ruler like the Clearview Triangle would be a worthwhile investment.

1. Start with a strip of fabric ¾″ wider than the size (height) of your finished triangle. Place the ruler on the strip of fabric. For this example I started with a 5″ strip for cutting triangles that will finish at 4¼″.

2. Cut off the excess on the left, and then cut the right-hand side to make your first triangle.

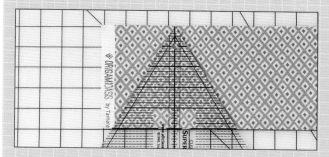

To save some time when I am cutting triangles, I slide my ruler down the strip of fabric to make my next cut. I line up the edge of the ruler so I can cut my second and third sets of triangles at the same time by cutting on both sides of the ruler.

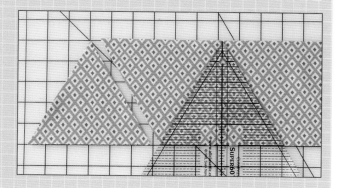

Hexagons

Problem ➤ My stitches are showing and my hexagons are pulling apart.

What you don't want:

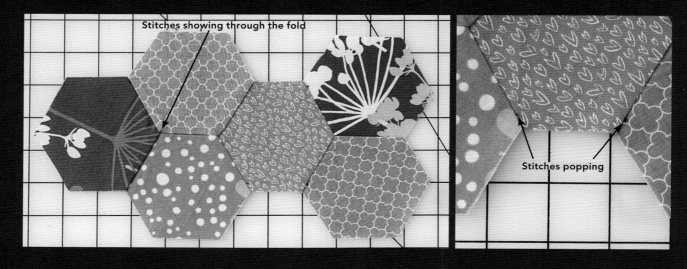

Stitches showing through the fold

Stitches popping

How your block should look:

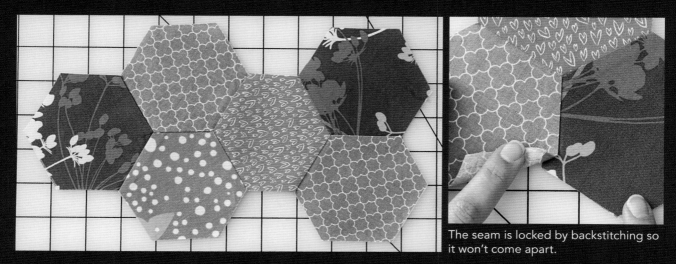

The seam is locked by backstitching so it won't come apart.

You did not mark the seam allowance or backstitch the Y-seams.

Hexagons are so popular right now. You can find a variety of precut hexagons at your local quilt shop, templates and rulers to cut them, specialty machines to cut them at home, and downloadable templates. Choose what works best for you or try a variety of techniques.

You can make amazing quilts using only Hexagon blocks or by incorporating hexagons into your quilt here and there. You can make hexagons in a variety of ways, too. I like to English paper piece smaller Hexagon blocks, but I find it easier to machine piece larger blocks.

> **Tip** You can also make a hexagon from six equilateral triangle units (page 98).

When I see flaws in hexagons that are pieced together, usually I can trace the problems back to a few causes—not marking and backstitching the seams, and not ironing properly. You have to clearly mark the seamline and make sure that you start and stop exactly at the end of the seam, backstitching to secure at both points. This is what makes Y-seams tricky.

I have tried to eyeball Y-seams and, while it works some of the time, it doesn't always, and I have to get out the seam ripper. To make sure you don't sew into your seam allowance, mark each hexagon ¼˝ from the edge. Use your favorite marking tool. I alternate between a quilting pencil and a water-soluble pen. Usually whatever I get my hands on first wins. Marking each intersection is a fair amount of work, but it will pay off when you don't have to take out stitches.

Use this method to sew hexagons and any other shapes that require Y-seams to keep the intersections flat.

1. Mark a ¼˝ seam allowance on each of your hexagons. You can save some time by marking only the corners.

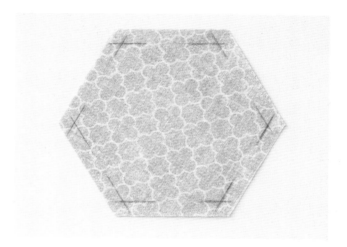

2. Place 2 hexagons right sides together. Place a pin through 2 adjacent corners of the hexagons. Make sure the pin goes through the marked corners on each side.

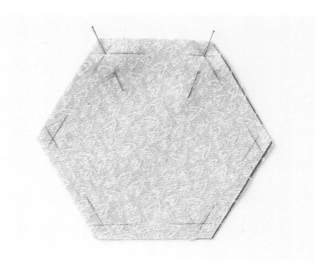

3. Sew between the pins, backstitching at each end of the seam. Be careful that your stitches don't go past the marked lines.

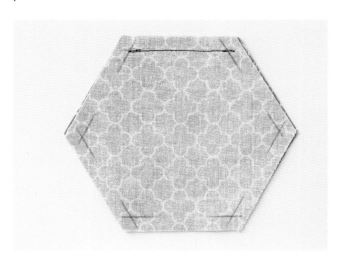

4. Open the Hexagon blocks. Place another hexagon on 1 block, right sides together.

5. Follow the process from Steps 3 and 4 to sew the next seam, adjacent to the first seam.

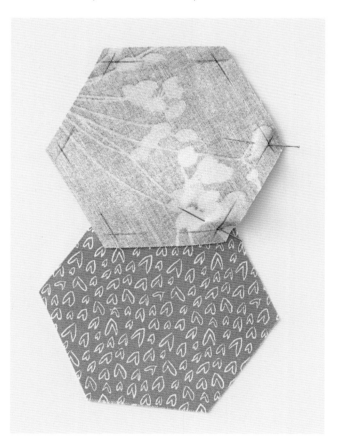

6. Open the hexagons. Notice that 2 sides of the block aren't sewn together yet.

7. Gently fold the hexagons so the 2 unsewn sides meet. Place a pin through each mark in the corner. Sew between the 2 pins. Backstitch and don't sew past the marked seam allowance.

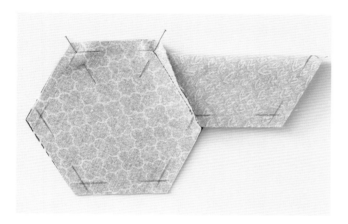
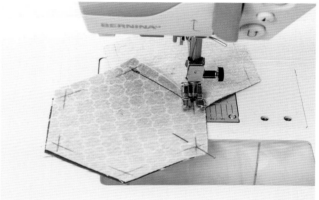

8. Place the hexagon unit right side down on your ironing board. Gently furl (page 27) the seam allowances at the center intersection by using your fingers to spread out the seam allowance. It will look like a tiny hexagon in the center. Press.

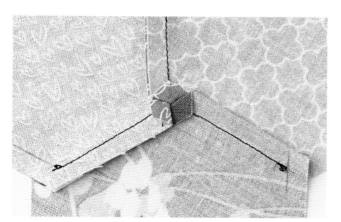
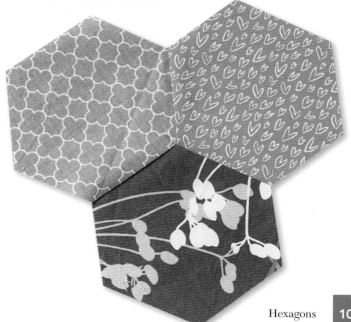

PREPARING HEXAGONS

One great tool for making Hexagons is the fast2cut HexEssentials Viewers (C&T Publishing). These sets contain several acrylic hexagon templates in a variety of sizes. The center of each hexagon is open, so the templates are great to use if you are fussy cutting pieces, but you can use them to cut any hexagon.

You can cut a strip of fabric, place your template on the strip, and cut hexagons,

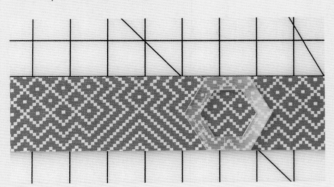

you can fussy cut pieces,

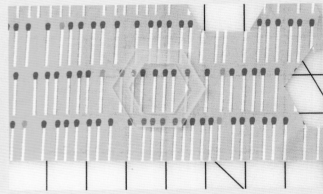

or you can cut hexagons from scraps.

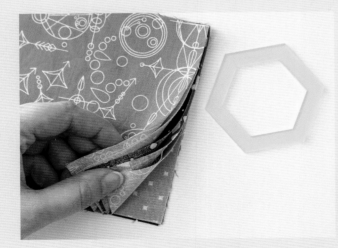

Once you determine where you want to cut, simply follow the outer edge of the template with your rotary cutter.

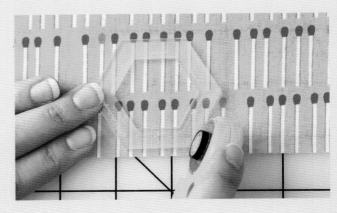

Because the center of the template is open, I like to draw the markings for my seams by tracing the inside of the template onto the back of my fabric. The HexEssentials templates have ⅜″ and ½″ seam allowances. The measurements are written on the templates, but it's easy to forget the seam allowance isn't ¼″. Drawing my seam allowance ensures that I won't make my hexagons too small.

This method allows me to easily mark my Y-seams with a pin before I sew, as in Step 2 of the Hexagons instructions (page 105), and ensures that I have beautifully pieced hexagons.

Diamonds

Problem ➤ The points of my diamonds don't match.

What you don't want:

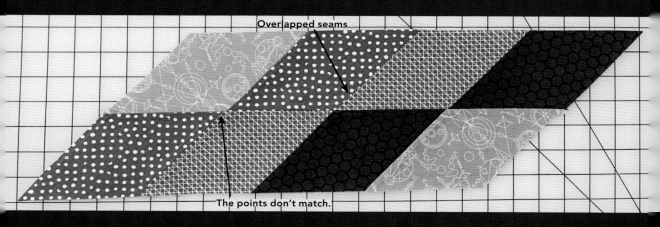

Overlapped seams

The points don't match.

How your block should look:

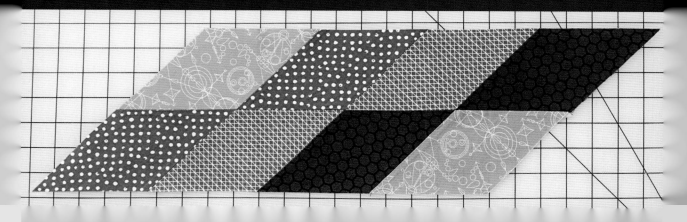

You didn't offset your seams enough to make the diamonds match, or the strip sets weren't perfectly pieced, causing mismatched points on the Diamond blocks.

SOLUTION

Normally when you piece a quilt, parts fit and seams nest together or match in some way. That's not the case with diamonds. In order to piece diamonds and have points that match, you have to offset your seams, meaning that your seamlines will fall in opposite directions. Before you pin rows of diamonds right sides together, be sure to mark each seamline at the ¼˝ seam allowance so you can match up the points with a pin.

You can buy templates for cutting diamonds individually, but I prefer to strip piece my diamonds together. It's easier and requires significantly less preparation. The smaller the strip, the smaller the diamond. I tend to work off the cuff, so I base the size of my diamonds on whatever strip size feels right. I recommend playing around with it a bit. You can always use a coping strip or another block in to fill space, or add more diamonds.

1. Sew several strips of fabric together to make your strip set. Press the seams open.

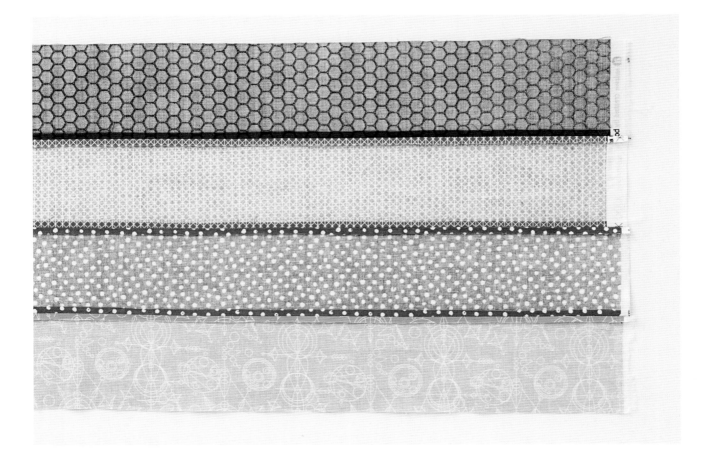

2. Place your ruler on the fabric with the 45° mark aligned with the bottom edge of the strip set. To waste as little fabric as possible, I try to place the top of the ruler at the very edge of the fabric and selvage.

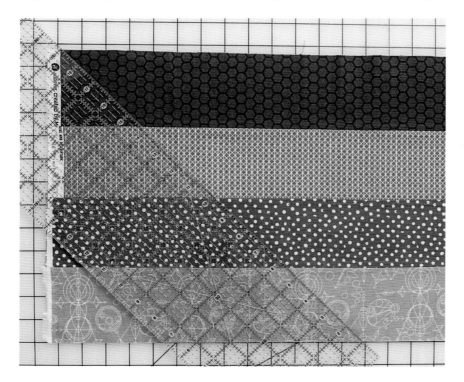

3. Make the first cut to remove excess from the left of the ruler. If you are left-handed, you may want to line up your ruler with the right-hand side of the fabric and cut from the opposite end.

4. Subcut rows of diamonds from the strip sets. Cut the rows the same width you cut the strips. If you cut 3½˝ strips, then cut 3½˝-wide rows of diamonds.

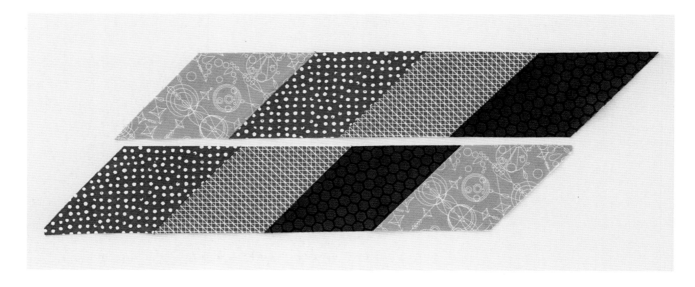

5. On the front of the fabric, lightly mark the ¼″ seam allowance at each seam.

6. Place 2 rows of diamonds right sides together. Use a pin to match the seams at the marked lines. Note that the seams face in opposite directions.

Tip Sometimes you may want to sew diamonds together, but without using strip sets. For example, you may want to attach a single diamond to a row or block, or you need to sew just a few diamonds together. If that's the case, mark and pin the ¼″ seam allowance at the points so you get perfect diamonds. You will know that you are sewing them correctly because you will have bunny ears.

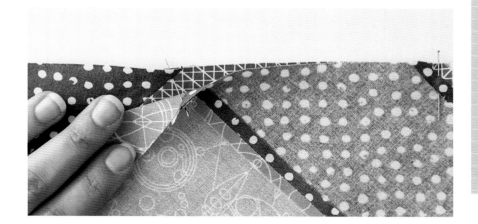

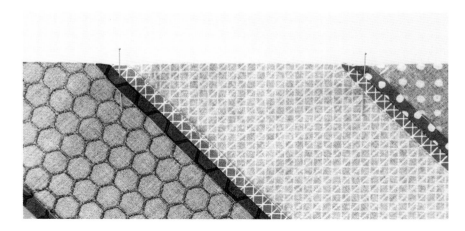

7. Sew the strips together. Set the seam and press it open.

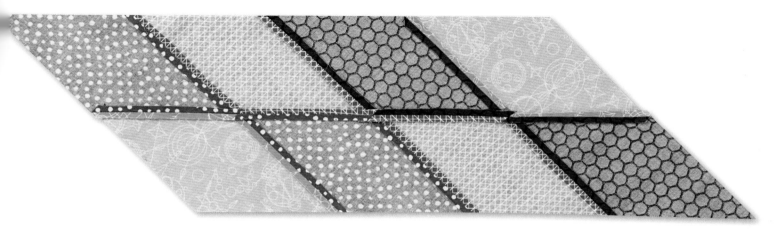

Kansas DUGOUT

Problem ➤ There is a pucker in my Y-seams, I have a stitch showing, and my template pieces don't match.

What you don't want:

Sewing into the ¼″ seam allowance creates a pucker.

The template pieces don't match.

How your block should look:

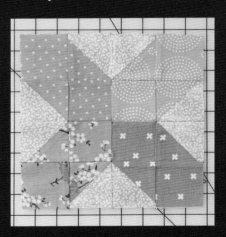

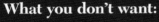

DIAGNOSIS

The traditional version of this block uses Y-seams and template-cut pieces, which need to be cut very accurately or your seams won't match. You sewed into the seam allowance, so your stitch shows through and causes puckering in the seam.

One of the things I love most about quilting is its versatility. Often there is more than one way to piece a block, and everyone has a favorite. One way isn't better than another unless it's better for you. I find that true of the Kansas Dugout block. The traditional block is made with templates, and the resulting octagon-shaped blocks are set together with small squares on point. The block construction requires a lot of Y-seams. When you sew Y-seams, it can be easy to accidentally stitch into the seam allowance, causing stitches to show on top of the block. If you aren't accurate when you cut the templates, your block can get wonky. If you would like to piece this block using templates and Y-seams, search online for free Kansas Dugout patterns, and see Hexagons (page 104) for information on how to correctly make a Y-seam.

I like a simplified approach. You can make the block template-free with squares and Half-Square Triangles (page 38).

1. For each quadrant of this block, you will need 2 squares of focus fabric and 2 half-square triangles made with the same focus fabric and a background fabric.

- The finished size of each half-square triangle and square will be ¼ of the finished size of the Kansas Dugout block. Press the seams of the half-square triangles open.

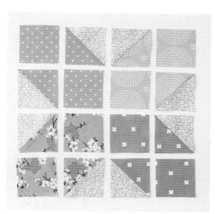

2. Sew each quadrant together Four-Patch style (page 34). Press the seams to one side.

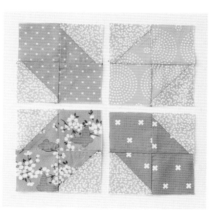

3. Sew 2 quadrants together to make 2 half-blocks. Press the seams to one side.

4. Sew the half-blocks together to complete the block.

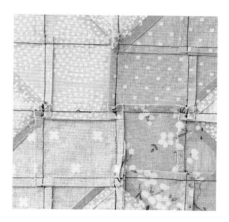

NOTE: I find that furling the seams helps the block lie flatter where the half-square triangles meet. However, one intersection wouldn't cooperate. Interestingly, it's much flatter than the other intersections were, so I left it (you can see where). I also want to show that often blocks just don't come out perfect. The best thing you can do for yourself, and your sanity, is to go with it.

PUTTING IT ALL TOGETHER

Piecing the top of your quilt is only half the battle when it comes to finishing, and this section discusses common problems. Pieces need to get squared up, borders need to get attached, setting triangles are needed if your quilt is set on point, and the list goes on. Separately those things are easy, but if you are new to quilting or intimidated by a part in the finishing process, it's easy to get overwhelmed.

I'll discuss a few tips to help manage problems when putting your top together. I'll tackle some math and offer creative solutions to common problems. The biggest limitation is you, so take these suggestions and make them work for your quilt.

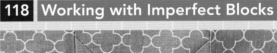

118 **Working with Imperfect Blocks**

120 Coping Strips

122 Sashings

126 Setting Triangles

130 Borders

140 Binding

Working WITH Imperfect Blocks

Problem I squared my block, but the seam allowance is less than ¼″ in some places.

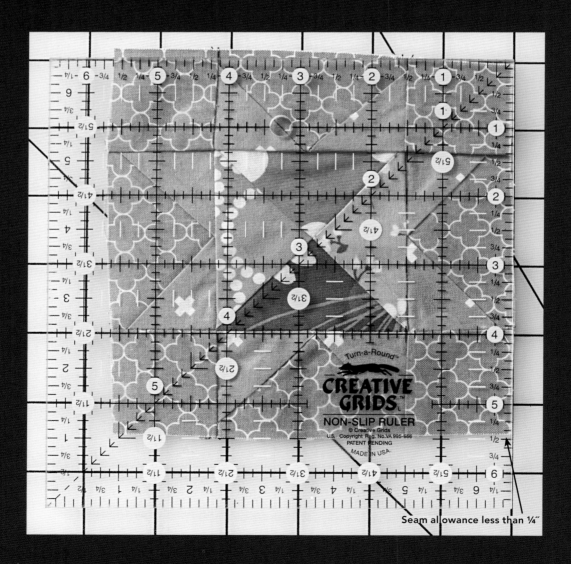

Seam allowance less than ¼″

Sometimes it just happens, and that's okay.

---------- **SOLUTION** ----------

Your points are perfect. Nothing has been chopped off. Even the center of your block is fantastic! The problem? You are human, and fabric shifts. Try as we might to make sure every square is perfect and no point is chopped off, at the end of the day some blocks never will be perfect. While that's not exactly what anyone wants to hear, there is a solution. Sew your block to something else.

For this example, I am sewing my block to a sashing strip, but you can just as easily sew it to another block, a border, or a coping strip. The possibilities are endless.

1. Place the straightest edge of the block onto a strip right sides together. Notice that the top of the block does not line up perfectly with the strip. That's okay.

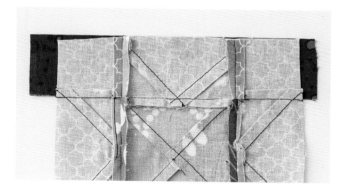

2. Draw a line ¼″ from the edge of the block. Notice that there is still plenty of fabric in the seam allowance. Even though the block isn't perfectly square, there is still enough fabric so you have an adequate seam allowance and you won't chop off your point. Pin the pieces together.

3. Sew, set the seam, and press the seam allowance toward the sashing.

NOTE: One challenge you may find is that your point doesn't quite meet the sashing. It's the tiniest bit off. My rule of thumb is that you are better off leaving a point floating than cutting it off. Usually it's barely noticeable.

Coping
STRIPS

Problem I want to put these blocks into a quilt, but they aren't the same size.

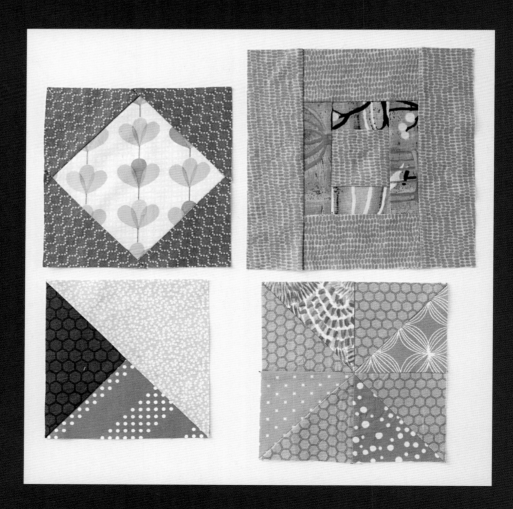

We've all had extra blocks pile up in our stash over the years. Sometimes they are test blocks we didn't use; sometimes friends give them to us. Either way, chances are they aren't the same size, and how do you make blocks fit together in a quilt if they aren't the same size? You use coping strips.

Coping strips are pieces of fabric that help you "cope" with different-sized blocks in your quilt. Coping strips can be strips of fabric, smaller blocks like half-square triangles or checkerboards, or any of a variety of shapes to make your blocks fit together. Striped and checkerboard fabrics are great for coping strips. They add a lot of interest without much work on your part.

When I use coping strips, I look at the blocks like a puzzle. I loosely arrange the blocks on my design wall in a pattern I like. Then I play with fabric strips, smaller blocks, and other design ideas to make everything fit.

NOTE: In the following photographs, I cut the strips to size to show you the finished look of blocks set together with coping strips. Please add seam allowances when you cut your coping strips.

1. Starting with 2 blocks is a good first place. You can build from there.

Notice that I added a striped piece of fabric to make the blocks fit together. It's less work than piecing a strip, and it adds interest to the blocks.

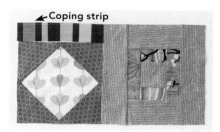

← Coping strip

Here I added 2 more blocks and set a block on point to get everything to fit. See Square-in-a-Square (page 56) for information on adding triangles to set a block on point.

This block is set on point.

2. If you look at the arrangement and don't like it, move blocks around and add more strips.

In addition to moving blocks around, I added some half-square triangles, some quarter-square triangles, a pieced checkerboard strip, and strips of fabric to make all the blocks fit.

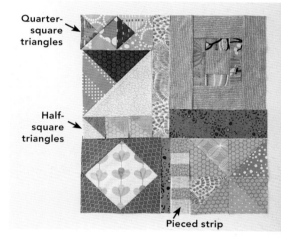

Quarter-square triangles

Half-square triangles

Pieced strip

I added a strip of orange here to make the layout a little more exciting.

Sashings

My sashings don't line up.

What you don't want:

How your quilt should look:

The sashing doesn't line up.

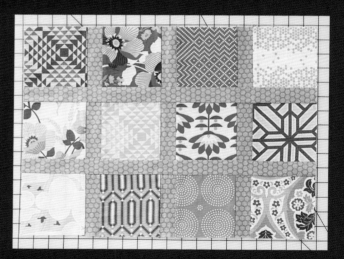

DIAGNOSIS

One of the rows shifted when you were sewing,
or you didn't line up the rows correctly before sewing them together.

Even with perfect blocks and piecing, mismatched sashings happen. It is frustrating to sew a few rows together only to see that the sashings don't match! This has definitely caused a headache or two for me before. If you do a little planning, pin, and manipulate the rows, you will have sashings sewn on straight in no time!

Be sure to press each row as you sew. As you press, check to see if the sashings are lined up. It is less frustrating to fix a row that you have just sewn than to see the problem when you think your quilt top is finished.

If you continue to have trouble lining up sashings, baste two rows together. You will be able to see if your rows match. If they don't, it's easy for you to remove the basting stitches and try again. If they are perfectly lined up, you can sew over the basting stitches.

I like to lay my rows on top of each other, right sides together, and then fold back the top and line up my sashings. I don't need a ruler or any fancy tools. Just my eyes!

1. Place 2 rows of your quilt together.

2. Put the top row facedown on the second row.

3. Carefully fold back the first few inches of the top row. Shift it to the right or left as needed to line up the sashings.

4. Pin the rows together, and then sew. Set the seam and press the seam allowances.

Tip If you follow the instructions for lining up your sashings and they still don't match, use this trick.

1. Align a ruler with the edge of a vertical sashing strip. Mark the top of the sashing row with your marking tool of choice.

2. Repeat for the other side of the sashing.

3. Use the marks as a guide to matching up the sashing with the blocks on the next row. Pin the rows together at each mark.

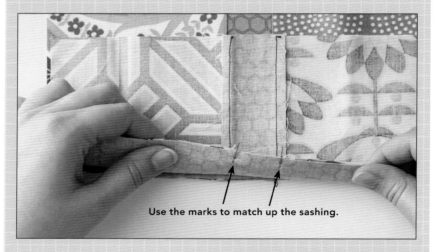

Use the marks to match up the sashing.

4. Sew the seam, easing in the longer side if necessary (page 22).

SASHING CORNERSTONE VARIATION

Adding cornerstones to your sashing really adds interest to your quilt. It is also easier to align the rows, because you can nest the seams of the cornerstones with the pieced blocks in the next row.

2. As you pin the rows together, nest the seams at the intersections (page 21) and pin. I like to pin each side of the cornerstone so the fabric doesn't shift as I'm sewing rows together.

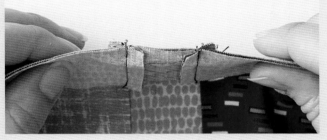

3. Sew the rows together. Set the seams and press as you go until the top is complete.

1. You will start with rows that look something like this.

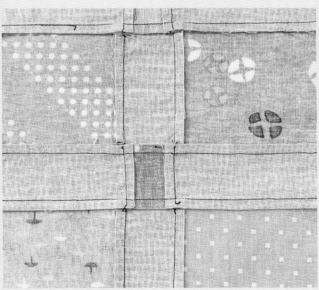

Tip If you use directional fabric for your sashing, make sure you cut strips on the lengthwise and crosswise grains so that all the strips end up going in the same direction. Having sashing fabric oriented in the same direction gives a custom look to your quilt.

Setting
TRIANGLES

Problem Some of my side setting triangles are too small and are wavy.

What you don't want:

How your quilt should look:

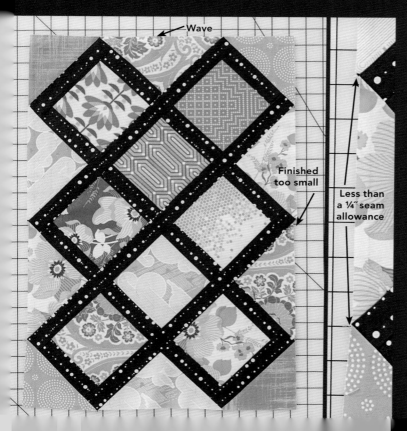

Wave

Finished too small

Less than a ¼" seam allowance

If you didn't calculate the setting triangle size to include the sashing, your triangle will be too small. If you cut the triangles so the bias edge is on the outside or you pulled on the triangles to make them fit, you will create a wave.

Take these steps to prevent waves on the edges of your quilt:

- Cut the triangles slightly larger than necessary and then trim them after you have sewn the quilt together.

- Be sure to take any sashings into account when you cut the side setting triangles. For example, if your finished squares are 4″ but you have a 1″ sashing, base the measurement on a 5″ square. Using the measurement of the finished blocks to determine what size to cut your side setting triangles without taking sashing into account will result in pieces that don't fit. Believe me, I've tried.

- Cut the corner and side setting triangles correctly, so that the bias edges of the triangles are on the inside of the quilt. This is crucial for making quilts with on-point settings because the straight grain of the fabric should be on the outer edge of the quilt. The corner setting triangles are cut from half-square triangles so the straight grain is on the outside of the quilt. The side setting triangles are quarter-square triangles, again placed with the straight grain on the outside of the quilt. Since the straight grain doesn't stretch as much as the bias, correct cutting and orientation should eliminate the wave in the edge of your quilt. Before cutting into your fabric, follow the simple equations to cut the corner and side setting triangles.

Tip You will have to sew along the bias edges of the corner and side setting triangles when you attach them to your quilt. Be careful not to stretch the pieces, and use lots of pins. The end result will be well worth the little bit of extra work.

1. Determine the size of your corner triangles. These are made using half-square triangles. Cut 2 squares, and then cut each in half diagonally to yield 4 corner triangles with the straight grain of the fabric on the outer edges. The equation is simple.

- Finished block size ÷ 1.414 = finished size of corner setting triangle

- Finished size of corner setting triangle + 1″ + ½″ = size of squares to cut

Following this method for making half-square triangles (page 38), I added 1″ plus an extra ½″ to give slightly oversized triangles that you can square up perfectly.

For example, to cut corner triangles for a quilt made with a 5″ finished block:

5″ ÷ 1.414 = 3.53″ (Usually I round up to the nearest ⅛″, but this is so close to 3½″ that I will use 3½″.)

3½″ + 1″ + ½″ = 5″

So cut the squares at 5″. Cut each square in half diagonally.

NOTE: If you use a directional fabric for the corner or side setting triangles, you may need to cut extra squares to yield enough triangles with the print oriented in the same direction. I like to orient the print in the same direction in each triangle. I do waste fabric, but the overall look is cleaner. I keep the extra triangles in an "extra parts box" for another project down the road.

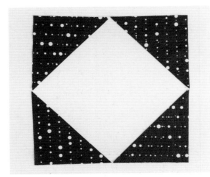

For the corner setting triangles, you can avoid wasting fabric by changing the direction of the diagonal cut. In these two squares of fabric, I made one diagonal cut from the lower left to the upper right, and the other from the lower right to the upper left. This way, the print will be oriented in the same direction for each corner setting triangle.

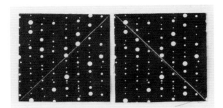

2. Determine the size of your side setting triangles. For these, you will cut a square in half diago-

nally in both directions to yield 4 triangles from each square. The straight grain runs along the long side of each triangle.

- finished block size × 1.414 = finished *long* side of side setting triangle

- finished long side of side setting triangle + 1½″ + ½″ = size of squares to cut

We added 1½″ because these are quarter-square triangles (page 40), and I add the extra ½″ to avoid the risk of having triangles that are too small.

For example, to cut side setting triangles for a quilt made with a 5″ finished block:

5″ × 1.414 = 7.07″, finished long side of side setting triangle (very close to 7″, so I will use 7″)

7″ + 1½″ + ½″ = 9″

So cut your squares at 9″. Cut each square on both diagonals to make 4 side setting triangles.

3. After you assemble the quilt top, square it up and trim the excess edges of the triangles using a square ruler in the corner and a 24″ ruler along the side.

NOTE: I like to use two rulers to square up my quilts, and I find I rarely have quilts that aren't square when I use this method. I place a square ruler at each corner to be sure that the corner is square, with a long ruler on the sides between the corners. It's been my experience that trying to square up a quilt without using a square ruler at the corners results in a quilt that is not quite square. If I rely only on a long ruler, often by the time I have moved the long ruler from the first corner to the next, the quilt is no longer totally square. With this method, I start with a perfectly square corner, and most of the time when I get to the opposite side of the edge, my cutting line is still straight. Getting points to match can get tricky, and from time to time you will have to move your ruler slightly to the right or left to make sure you are still square.

Start by putting a square ruler in the corner, ¼″ from the edge of the blocks.

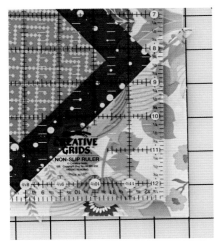

The excess triangle fabric to the right and bottom of the ruler is still relatively square with the edge of the quilt.

4. Place the 24″ ruler on top of the square ruler. Make sure that the ¼″ mark is lined up next to the points along the outside edge of your quilt. If the rulers and the quilt are lined up perfectly, then the lines of the rulers will fall directly on top of each other and you can trim along the side of the perfectly aligned rulers. In this example, however, they don't line up. If this happens to you, follow the technique in Step 5 to trim the side.

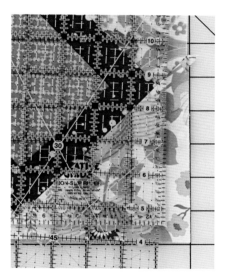

The square ruler is ¼″ from the point on the bottom and ¼″ from the point on the side. Now, look at the yellow ruler. Notice that the 45° line is parallel with the dark gray sashing. If the rulers and quilt lined up perfectly, then the lines on the rulers would fall directly on each other, but they don't.

5. Start cutting from the edge of the square ruler to the spot where the square ruler and the long ruler meet.

6. Follow the long ruler until you get near the next corner, then repeat the 2-ruler process. Make sure you give yourself enough

space at the following corner to line up the square ruler.

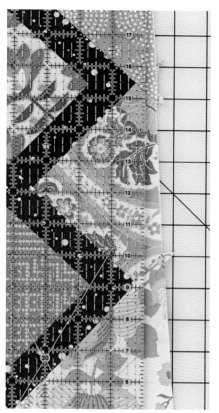

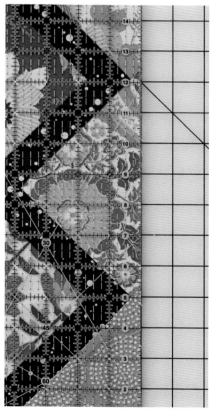

7. Continue to work your way around the quilt to square up and trim each corner and the remaining sides.

Tip **Basting Bias Edges**

From time to time, you may not have enough fabric to make all the setting triangles with the straight grain along the outside edge. If you have just enough fabric to cut triangles with the outer edges on the bias, go ahead, but take care. The trick is to baste the edges of the quilt to keep the fabric from stretching or distorting.

Baste each side separately instead of stitching around the corners. Leave a tail of thread several inches long at the end of each side. Basting will cause the slightest bit of gathering in your quilt top. To flatten the quilt, smooth the gathers by sliding the extra fabric onto the thread tails.

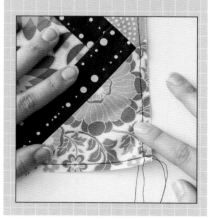

Borders

Problem ➤ The seams of my pieced border are pulling apart.

What you don't want:

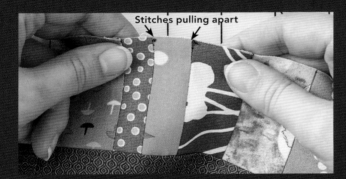

Stitches pulling apart

How your pieced border should look:

DIAGNOSIS

Pieced quilt borders have a lot of seams on the outer edges. If you pull the seams when piecing or basting, the stitches will pop, leaving you with a wonky edge or a quilt that comes apart.

SOLUTION

Every so often I like to make a quilt border from scraps or I make a quilt that just needs a pieced border, like piano keys. Pieced borders add interest, use leftover fabric, and coordinate perfectly. I've done it a time or two when I wanted to finish up a quilt and my local quilt shop wasn't open (read: It was late at night). Whatever your reason, pieced borders are fun!

Unfortunately, if there is drag on the quilt when you are putting on the borders, or if you handle the scrappy borders too much, they will pull apart. I've even seen stitches pop as the quilt is being basted for quilting. If you don't want to backstitch each time you reach the outer edge of your pieced border, baste each edge of the quilt after you have added the pieced borders. This will keep stitches from popping.

Problem ➤ My borders are wavy.

What you don't want:

Waves in the border

How your quilt should look:

- - - - - - - - - - - - - - - **DIAGNOSIS** - - - - - - - - - - - - - - -

If you don't cut your borders the correct size before piecing them to your quilt, you will create a wave.

- - - - - - - - - - - - - - - **SOLUTION** - - - - - - - - - - - - - - -

Nobody wants a wave in a quilt border. Even if you can quilt it out—and you can't always—it's a pain. This can be particularly problematic if your border strips are cut on the crosswise grain and sewn into a long strip, because the crosswise grain is slightly stretchy and can contribute to the wave.

To prevent this from happening, cut your borders based on measurements taken at the center of the quilt. The measurement at the quilt center is

usually more accurate and will help you keep your quilt square. I measure and cut my inner borders this way, too.

You can piece the borders on the side or the top first. It's a personal preference. See what you like best. Sometimes it depends on the border fabric. If I have a directional fabric, I can buy a little less yardage if I piece the sides first. If I miter the corners, it doesn't matter which borders I sew on first.

1. Place the quilt on a flat surface and smooth out any wrinkles. Place a tape measure across the center of your quilt to get the length for the first 2 borders. Cut the borders.

2. Place each border on opposite sides of the qulit. For each border, pin the center of the border to the center of the quilt side, and then pin the ends. Ease in where necessary.

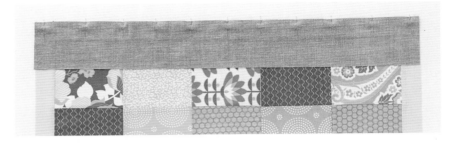

3. Sew the borders to the quilt. Set the seam and press the seam allowances toward the borders.

5. For the 2 remaining sides, pin the center of the border to the center of the quilt side, and then pin the ends. Ease in where necessary.

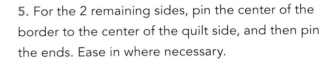

4. Lay the quilt on a flat surface. Smooth out any wrinkles and measure across the center to get the length for the other 2 borders. Cut the borders.

6. Sew the remaining 2 borders to the quilt. Set the seams and press toward the borders.

Problem ➤ The prints on my quilt borders are oriented in different directions.

What you don't want:

The border design changes direction at the corners.

How your quilt should look:

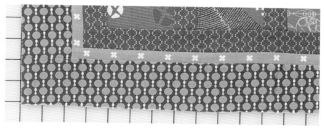

DIAGNOSIS

You cut all the border strips in one direction, resulting in border strips that appear to intersect with each other.

SOLUTION

It's not the worst thing in the world to have border prints going in different directions, but your quilt deserves better. Looking at a quilt with borders that don't come close to matching is the equivalent of hearing nails on a chalkboard for me. I think it's a visual assault on my senses. I'm not saying they have to be absolutely perfect, because sometimes that's

not possible, but close and having the same orientation is good enough for me. There may be cases where changing the orientation is what you want, for example with a striped border. However, for fabrics with a directional print, quilts just look better when the directional borders are oriented in the same direction.

Usually fabric is printed so the pattern follows the lengthwise grain of the fabric. Cut the side borders along the length of the fabric, and cut the top and bottom borders on the width of the fabric. This will give you border pieces that are oriented in the same direction as your quilt. Depending on the orientation of the print, you may have to cut the side borders on the width of fabric and the top and bottom borders on the length of fabric.

1. Determine the direction you want to cut the borders. For this example, I wanted the pink and white lines to run vertically.

2. Measure the center of your quilt to determine the length of the border. Cut the borders along the lengthwise grain of the fabric. For larger quilts, you will need to move your ruler with the fabric to get the correct length. Do not include the selvage in the border.

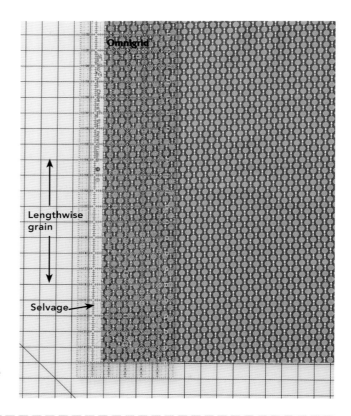

3. Sew a border to each side of the quilt. Refer to Problem: My Borders Are Wavy (page 131) for instructions on how to attach borders.

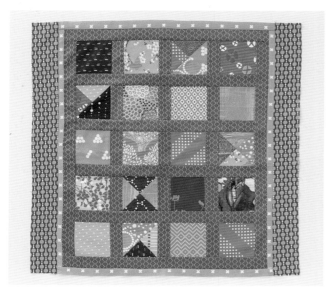

4. Measure the center of your quilt to determine the length for the other 2 borders.

5. Cut the remaining borders on the crosswise grain of the fabric.

6. Sew the borders to the top and bottom of the quilt.

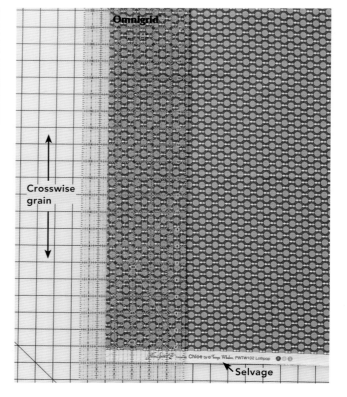

DIRECTIONAL PRINT ALTERNATIVES

Cutting Solutions

While it would be ideal to cut all borders along the grain of the fabric, it's not always possible. You would have to buy yards of fabric, and not everyone wants that expense or the extra fabric that is left over, though it's great to use for the back of your quilt. Instead, you can buy a smaller amount of fabric and piece strips together.

For example, let's say you have a quilt that needs a 4″ × 50½″ border but you don't want to buy 1½ yards (54″) of fabric. You can buy 1 yard of fabric (36″) and cut 2 strips on the lengthwise grain, 4½″ × 25½″ each. Piece together the 2 strips to make your border.

Or, you can make your borders from a section that is 10½″ × width of fabric. Cut 5 lengthwise strips at 4½″ × 10½″ and sew them together to make each side border.

You can miter the seam or sew it straight across. Either is fine. It really is a matter of personal preference. A mitered seam wastes a little fabric but can sometimes be less noticeable. That's not always the case with larger prints, so consider your fabric print before deciding to sew a mitered seam. A straight seam is less wasteful, and sometimes it is easier to match prints.

Mitered seams often add interest to quilts, but they do require more fabric. If you miter a seam or corner, you need to add the width of your strip twice to the length of whatever you are sewing. For example, if you want a mitered seam for a border that finishes at 4″ × 50½″, cut 2 strips 4½″ wide with lengths totaling 58½″. Mitering corners requires more fabric and greater precision in sewing. You can add another 5″–6″ to your border to make sure you have plenty of fabric for your mitered seams.

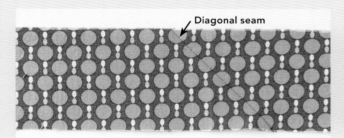

Mitered border strip

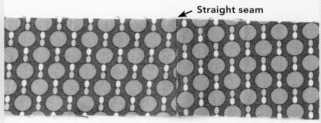

Border strip sewn straight across

Mitered Corners

You can miter the corners of your border strips, too.

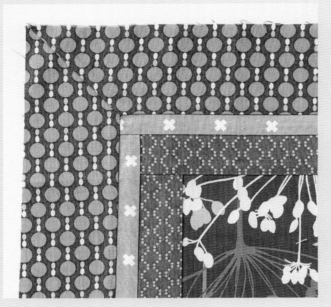

1. Cut each border strip long enough to overlap the other by the width of the adjacent border, and then add another ½˝. For example, if you want mitered corners for a border that finishes at 4˝ × 50½˝, cut 2 strips 4½˝ × 59˝. Mitering corners requires more fabric and greater precision in sewing. You can add another 5˝–6˝ to your border to make sure you have plenty of fabric for your mitered seams.

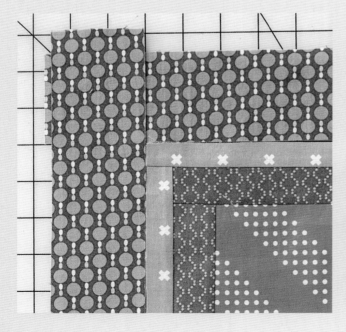

Mark both the quilt and the border strips at the center, and mark each border strip at a point at each end that matches the quilt side to which it will be sewn, minus ¼˝. Pin the border to the quilt, matching the marks on the border to the marks on the quilt that are ¼˝ from the edges. The pins will show you exactly where to stop and backstitch to make a mitered corner.

2. Sew a strip to 2 adjacent sides of the quilt, stopping ¼˝ from the edge. Backstitch at the corner so the border strips don't pull away from the quilt top. Notice that the backstitched seams don't intersect. You want that. If your seams overlap you will create a pleat in the front.

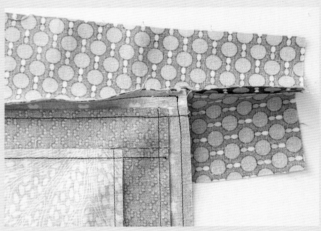

3. Fold the corner of the quilt at a 45° angle, aligning the border edges.

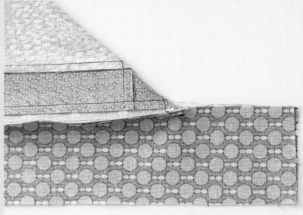

4. Align a ruler with the folded edge of the quilt, as shown.

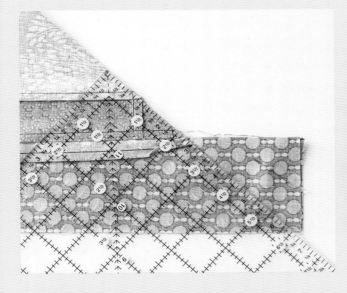

5. Draw a line from the end of the stitches on your border to the outer edge. Pin the borders together.

6. Sew along the line. Backstitch where the border meets the quilt top. Set the seam, trim, and press open.

Border Cornerstones

If you want to use a directional print but don't want to miter the corners or don't have enough fabric, use a cornerstone! Cornerstones add interest to your quilt and they will create distance between border prints with different orientations.

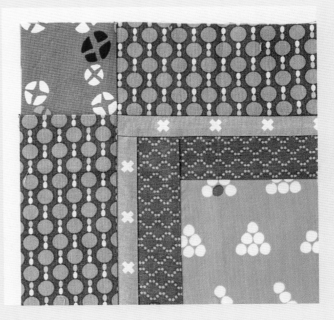

What you don't want:

- - - - - - - - - - - - - - - - - - - **SOLUTION** - - - - - - - - - - - - - - - - - - -

It always happens late at night. You don't have enough of the perfect fabric for your border that you bought five years ago and you know you can't find any more of it. Nothing is more frustrating than coming up short for your borders.

Instead of buying more fabric, play with what you have at home. Fortunately, necessity is the mother of all creativity. I always tell my students to experiment with different solutions until they find one they like. Borders do not have to be single strips of fabric. Often what you create out of necessity is better than the original concept, anyhow.

In the following mockups, see how each possible solution changes the look of the quilt.

Add cornerstones if you are a tiny bit short on fabric.

Create dimension by using two different fabrics and mitered seams.

Extend the center of your quilt into the border for some interest.

Use the perfect fabric as an inner border and continue the sashing fabric on the outer border.

I've given you a few ideas, but the possibilities are endless. Be creative and have fun!

Binding

Problem ➤ My curved binding corners are rolling back.

What you don't want:

How your curved corner should look:

The binding rolls back.

DIAGNOSIS

You pulled the bias binding too tight as you sewed around the curve.

Curved corners are a fun look for quilts, and they are great for baby quilts that get dragged around. Bias binding goes around curved corners so easily, but if you pull it too tight when you are sewing it onto the quilt, the binding will roll under the quilt. It's not a good look.

To prevent that from happening, pin the binding to the curve before sewing it down. If the binding is pinned, you are less likely to pull it taut. You may have some wave on the outer edge of the binding, but that's normal and will go away when you fold the binding to the back.

1. Pin the binding around the corner of your quilt. If you are new to this, you cannot use too many pins.

2. Notice that there is wave in the folded edge of the binding, but the binding at the outside edge of the quilt is smooth.

3. Sew the binding to the quilt, removing pins as you go. See how it flips up? That's normal, and when you fold the binding to the back of the quilt, the wave will disappear.

4. Fold and stitch the binding to the back of the quilt.

Tip I like to sew my bindings down by hand. Make sure you sew with your stitches close together—close enough that a baby's fingers won't tear them apart.

What you don't want:

How your corner should look:

Corner not mitered

- - - - - - - - - - - - - - - - - - - **DIAGNOSIS** -

You didn't put a fold in your binding as you sewed it to the quilt.

- - - - - - - - - - - - - - - - - - - **SOLUTION** -

For years, I have had students tell me how much the corners of bindings intimidate them. Mitering the corners of binding actually is nothing more than a few flips, some folds, and one small but well placed line of stitches.

1. Sew the binding to a side of the quilt, stopping ¼″ from the edge, and then sew up to the corner at a 45° angle. I usually eyeball it, but if you are just starting, mark your quilt with a pin. This row of stitches will make it easy to fold back your binding to make a miter.

2. Flip the binding up, along the little seam you just stitched, to make a 45° angle.

3. Fold the binding back down on itself, with the fold aligned with the top edge of the quilt.

Sew up to the corner at 45°.

4. Sew a straight line from the top of the binding to the next corner, and repeat for the remaining sides.

NOTE: When you fold the binding to the back of the quilt, you will create a 45° angle on the front corner and on the back corner. When you stitch down the folded edge of the binding, stitch the mitered edges closed, by hand or by machine.

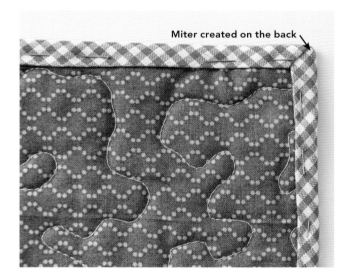

Miter created on the back

To decrease bulk, make sure that the fold in the binding on the back goes in the opposite direction from the fold on the front.

About the Author

Photo by Greg Scott, Picture This! Photography

Patty Murphy has been sewing since she was six years old. The first thing she recalls making is a pink-and-white seersucker pillow with the word *Dad* crudely embroidered on it as a gift for her father on Father's Day. Fortunately for everyone, her sewing and quilting have greatly improved since then, and so has her gift giving.

Patty loves to share her craft with anyone that will listen, and she teaches regularly at Intown Quilters in Decatur, Georgia, so she can share her knowledge and support her fabric obsession. Her work has been featured in several books, on the websites of major fabric manufacturers, on blogs, and in magazines, including an original quilt design for Intown Quilters that was featured on the cover of the Spring 2007 *Quilt Sampler* magazine.

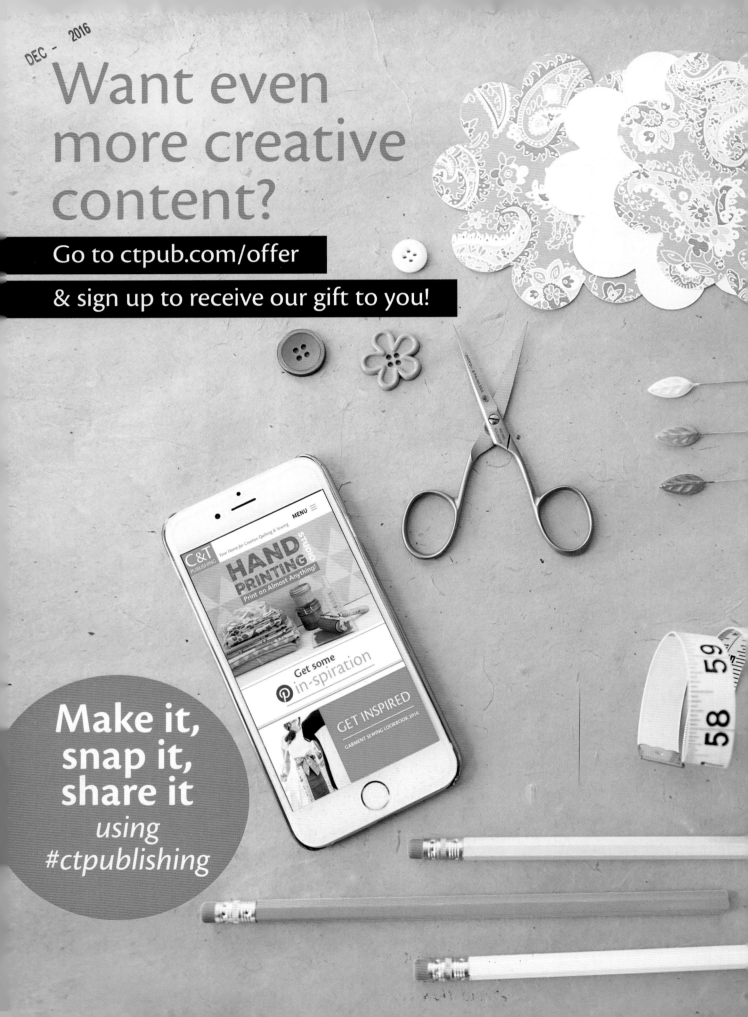